FREEDOM FIGHTERS

HEROES OF FAITH
WHO STOOD FOR TRUTH

MOSES ★ ESTHER ★ DANIEL ★ PAUL ★ JESUS

A 42-DAY DEVOTIONAL JOURNEY
Featuring Powerful Daily Personal Prayers
and Prayers for Your Nation

CYRIL OPOKU

Freedom Fighters: Heroes of Faith Who Stood for Truth

Freedom Fighters: Heroes of Faith Who Stood for Truth
    Featured Heroes:
1. Moses: The Deliverer in the Desert (7-Day Devotional)
2. Esther: Courage in the Shadows (8-Day Devotional)
3. Daniel: Standing Tall in a Fallen World (9-Day Devotional)
4. Paul: Faith That Can't Be Locked Down (9-Day Devotional)
5. Jesus: The Ultimate Freedom-Giver (9-Day Devotional)

© 2025 Cyril Opoku. BiblePlan™ Devotionals by TeenCompass Collective. All rights reserved.

No part of this book may be reproduced, stored in a retrieval system, or transmitted in any form or by any means—electronic, mechanical, photocopying, recording, or otherwise—without the prior written permission of the publisher, except for brief quotations used in reviews, articles, or other non-commercial purposes as permitted by copyright law.

All Scripture quotations, unless otherwise indicated, are taken from:

Scripture quotations marked (NIV) are taken from the Holy Bible, New International Version®, NIV®. Copyright ©1973, 1978, 1984, 2011 by Biblica, Inc.™ Used by permission. All rights reserved worldwide.

Scripture quotations marked (ESV) are taken from the ESV® Bible (The Holy Bible, English Standard Version®), copyright © 2001 by Crossway, a publishing ministry of Good News Publishers. Used by permission. All rights reserved.

Scripture quotations marked (NKJV) are taken from the New King James Version®.

Copyright © 1982 by Thomas Nelson. Used by permission. All rights reserved.

Published by *Quest Publications (questpublications@outlook.com)*

Cover design & Interior layout by *Quest Publications*

ISBN: 978-1-988439-54-9

Printed in the United States of America

First Edition: June 2025

For more devotionals by BiblePlan™ Devotionals visit TeenCompass Collective: https://teencompasscollective.org

Contents

PART 1—Moses: The Deliverer in the Desert

Day 1.	Born for a Purpose	2
Day 2.	The Fight Before the Freedom	5
Day 3.	The Call from the Fire	8
Day 4.	No More Excuses	11
Day 5.	When Courage Meets Resistance	14
Day 6.	The Power Behind the Mission	17
Day 7.	Freedom Walks Forward	20

PART 2—Esther: Courage in the Shadows

Day 8.	God's Hand in Hidden Places	24
Day 9.	Positioned with a Purpose	27
Day 10.	When Evil Has a Platform	30
Day 11.	For Such a Time as This	33
Day 12.	The Power of a Pause	36
Day 13.	Flip the Script	39
Day 14.	Justice Comes	42
Day 15.	From Surviving to Thriving	45

PART 3—Daniel: Standing Tall in a Fallen World

| Day 16. | Exiled, Not Forsaken | 50 |

Day 17.	Conviction Over Compromise	53
Day 18.	The God Who Knows All	56
Day 19.	The God Who Sees Tomorrow	59
Day 20.	Courage in the Fire	62
Day 21.	The Courage to Speak, the Grace to Bow	65
Day 22.	The Writing on the Wall	68
Day 23.	Standing Strong When It Counts	71
Day 24.	A Kingdom That Cannot Fall	74

PART 4—Paul: Faith That Can't Be Locked Down

Day 25.	Arrested by Grace	78
Day 26.	Unshakable Joy in the Chains	81
Day 27.	The Mission Doesn't Pause	84
Day 28.	Faith on Trial	87
Day 29.	Courage in the Chaos	90
Day 30.	Preaching Under Guard	93
Day 31.	Strength in Weakness	96
Day 32.	Joy No Matter What	99
Day 33.	Finishing Strong	102

PART 5—Jesus: The Ultimate Freedom-Giver

Day 34.	The Promise of Freedom	106
Day 35.	Freedom from Shame	109
Day 36.	Freedom from Religion	112

Day 37.	Freedom from Fear	115
Day 38.	Freedom from Sin's Grip	118
Day 39.	Freedom through the Cross	121
Day 40.	Freedom through Resurrection	124
Day 41.	Freedom to Live Changed	127
Day 42.	Freedom That Lasts Forever	130

Preface

We live in a world where truth is often challenged, courage is rare, and standing firm in faith can feel like swimming upstream. Yet throughout history, God has raised up men and women who didn't back down—people who stood for what was right, even when it was costly. This book is a tribute to them.

Freedom Fighters: Heroes of Faith Who Stood for Truth is more than a devotional—it's a call to courage. Within these pages, you'll walk alongside five biblical figures who faced overwhelming odds, yet remained faithful to God's calling on their lives. From Moses' deliverance in the desert to Esther's bravery in the palace, from Daniel's boldness in Babylon to Paul's unwavering faith in prison—and ultimately, to Jesus, the true and final freedom-giver—each story challenges us to live with conviction in our own generation.

This book is divided into five devotional journeys. Each one focuses on a single hero of faith, highlighting the spiritual battles they faced, the choices they made, and the God who empowered them. Whether you're reading this as a personal study, a family devotional, or a small group guide, my prayer is that each day inspires you to stand firm, speak truth, and trust God—no matter the cost.

In an age that often rewards compromise, may these devotionals help you rise as a freedom fighter for God's kingdom.

Stand firm. Speak boldly. Live freely.

— Cyril O. (June 2025)

Introduction

Freedom Worth Fighting For

Every year on the Fourth of July, Americans celebrate their national independence with fireworks, parades, and patriotic songs. It's a day that honors the hard-won freedom from tyranny and oppression—a reminder that liberty is a precious gift that should never be taken for granted. But long before any constitution was written or any flag was raised, there was a greater freedom story already being told—a story written by God.

The Bible is filled with men and women who fought for truth, not with swords or politics, but with faith, courage, and obedience to God. Their victories weren't always visible. Many didn't live to see the full reward of their sacrifices. Yet they stood firm in a world determined to silence them. They were *freedom fighters*—not for a nation, but for a kingdom that cannot be shaken.

This devotional book is about five of those heroes: Moses, Esther, Daniel, Paul, and Jesus. Each faced their own kind of battle. Each had to choose between comfort and courage, silence and truth, fear and faith. Their lives still speak today—not just to Americans, but to people in every nation who long to live free in a world that often demands compromise.

True freedom isn't found in flags or governments—it's found in the presence of God, in the truth of His Word, and in the courage to obey Him no matter the cost. Whether you live in a land of liberty or a place of persecution, this truth remains: **Christ has set us free** (Galatians 5:1).

So as you read these devotionals, don't just remember the past—rise to the present. Be inspired by those who went before you. And let God ignite in you the same fire that burned in their hearts: the fire to stand for truth, to live for eternity, and to fight for the kind of freedom that can never be taken away.

What You Can Expect

Each day of this devotional follows a simple but powerful structure designed to guide your heart, engage your mind, and stir your spirit:

- **Title & BiblePlan Reading** – The main theme of the day and the Scripture passage to read.
- **Focus** – A one-sentence summary of the core message.
- **Ponder** – A reflection question to help personalize the theme.
- **Key Verse(s)** – A highlighted Scripture to memorize or meditate on.
- **Devotional Reading** – A heartfelt, Scripture-based reflection that draws timeless truth from the hero's story and connects it to your life.
- **Personal Prayer** – A guided prayer for surrender, strength, or purpose.
- **Prayer for the Nation** – A short intercessory prayer for your country or the world.
- **Memorable Quote** – A truth to remember and share.

- **Reflection Questions** – Three prompts for journaling, group discussion, or deeper thought.

This layout is designed to be used daily—whether during your quiet time, over coffee with a friend, or with a small group. It's intentionally relevant, rooted in Scripture, and rich with practical application.

May this devotional awaken courage in you—not just to read about heroes of faith, but to become one. You were born into this generation *on purpose*. The same God who called Moses from a basket, Esther from obscurity, Daniel from exile, Paul from chains, and Jesus to the cross… now calls *you* to rise, speak, serve, and live free.

Let their stories inspire yours.

Part 1

MOSES: THE DELIVERER IN THE DESERT

A 7-Day Journey on Deliverance, Courage, and Calling

Discover how Moses' life shows us what it means to answer God's call, face fear with faith, and fight for freedom—not just politically, but spiritually.

Memory Verse:
"The Lord will fight for you; you need only to be still."
— Exodus 14:14 (NIV)

Day 1

Born for a Purpose

BiblePlan Reading: Exodus 2:1–10

Focus: Even before Moses could speak, God had a plan for him. His life was preserved for a greater mission.

Ponder: What has God preserved you for?

Key Verse(s): *"When she saw that he was a fine child, she hid him for three months."*—Exodus 2:2b (ESV)

Before Moses ever stood before Pharaoh, parted a sea, or led a nation to freedom, he was a helpless baby born into a time of crisis. Pharaoh's decree meant death for every Hebrew baby boy. But God's plan was stronger than Egypt's fear. Hidden by his mother, protected in a basket, and drawn from the river by Pharaoh's own daughter—Moses' life was not only preserved, it was positioned for purpose.

Even as an infant, Moses was caught in the clash between oppression and deliverance. But God was already at work. The same God who saw the suffering of His people also saw the child through whom He would bring freedom. This is a powerful reminder: when the world feels hostile, when injustice seems overwhelming, God is still shaping deliverers in hidden places.

Moses didn't earn his calling—it was grace. And so is yours. You may not feel like a "freedom fighter," but God has preserved you for more than survival. He's preserved you for impact. Your life has a mission that stretches beyond comfort or success. Whether it's standing for truth in a culture of compromise, defending the vulnerable, or simply choosing faith over fear, your presence in this generation is not an accident.

God raises up people in every generation to confront injustice with courage. Today, that includes you.

PERSONAL PRAYER:

> God, thank You for preserving my life with purpose. Just like You watched over Moses, I trust that You are guiding my path. Give me courage to live boldly for You, to stand for truth and justice, and to embrace the mission You've placed before me. Use my life to bring freedom and hope to others. In Jesus' name, Amen.

PRAYER FOR THE NATION:

Father God, we come before You acknowledging that true freedom and justice come only through Your perfect timing and wisdom. Forgive us when we act hastily or rely on our own strength to fix what only You can heal. Soften our hearts and guide our nation toward humility, patience, and faithfulness. Raise up leaders and citizens who will stand courageously for truth, seeking Your guidance above all else. Prepare us in every trial, just as You prepared Moses, so that we may walk boldly in the freedom You have called us to. Amen.

MEMORABLE QUOTE:

"God doesn't just preserve lives—He positions them for purpose."

REFLECTION:

1. What has God preserved you for? What threats or trials has God brought you through—and what might He be preparing you for?
2. Where can you begin to stand for truth and justice in your community or relationships?
3. How can you daily live with the awareness that you were born for a greater mission?

Day 2

The Fight Before the Freedom

BiblePlan Reading: Exodus 2:11–25

Focus: Moses' passion for justice was real, but he acted in haste. His calling needed time and God's refining.

Ponder: Do you ever try to "fix" things in your own strength?

Key Verse(s): *"He looked this way and that, and seeing no one, he struck down the Egyptian and hid him in the sand."*—Exodus 2:12 (ESV)

Moses saw the injustice. He saw his fellow Hebrew being beaten and couldn't stay silent. His heart burned with a desire to make things right. But in his youthful zeal, Moses took matters into his own hands—and it cost him everything. Instead of becoming a hero, he became a fugitive. Instead of leading a revolution, he ran into the wilderness.

This passage reveals a vital truth: passion without preparation can be dangerous. Moses wasn't wrong to care about injustice. In fact, that fire for justice was part of his God-given calling. But the method mattered. Moses needed more than passion—he needed God's timing, God's wisdom, and God's refining.

How many of us try to bring about change in our own way, in our own strength? Whether it's a family issue, a cultural injustice, or a personal burden, we often rush into "fix-it" mode without seeking the Lord. But spiritual freedom doesn't come by force—it comes through faith. And God often prepares His deliverers in the desert before He sends them to the front lines.

In God's mercy, Moses' failure wasn't the end of the story. It was part of the shaping process. God didn't abandon him—He redirected him. Forty years in the desert didn't cancel Moses' calling. It prepared him for it.

God still works that way. Your failure isn't final. If you've acted in haste, take heart—God can redeem even your missteps and refine your passion into purpose.

PERSONAL PRAYER:

> Lord, I confess that sometimes I rush ahead, trying to fix things my way instead of trusting Yours. Refine my heart. Shape my passion into Your purpose. Teach me to wait for Your timing and to fight for freedom with wisdom, not just emotion. In Jesus' name, amen.

Prayer for the Nation:

Lord, we ask You to guide our nation with Your wisdom and justice. Help us to resist rushing ahead in our own strength and instead trust Your perfect timing and plan. Refine our hearts so that our passion for freedom and justice aligns with Your truth and mercy. Raise up humble leaders who seek You first, and use us all to bring healing, hope, and lasting peace. Amen.

Memorable Quote:

"A calling from God is not just about what burns in your heart—but how long you're willing to let Him refine it."

Reflection:

1. Where have you acted in your own strength instead of waiting on God?
2. What "desert season" might God be using to prepare you for your true calling?
3. How can you begin to surrender your passion to God's process today?

Day 3

The Call from the Fire

BiblePlan Reading: Exodus 3:1–22

Focus: God speaks to Moses from a burning bush—calling him not just to go, but to *go with God*.

Ponder: What might God be calling you to do that feels too big?

Key Verse(s): *"Then the Lord said, 'I have surely seen the affliction of my people who are in Egypt and have heard their cry... Come, I will send you to Pharaoh that you may bring my people... out of Egypt.'"* —Exodus 3:7,10 (ESV)

Moses wasn't searching for a divine encounter—he was tending sheep in the wilderness. But God broke through the ordinary with something extraordinary: a bush on fire that didn't burn out. From this unexplainable sight came an unmistakable call. God didn't just speak; He invited Moses into His mission—to confront injustice, to lead a nation to freedom, and to trust that God Himself would go with him.

Moses immediately felt unqualified. "Who am I that I should go to Pharaoh?" (v. 11). But God's response didn't flatter Moses—it focused on Himself: *"But I will be with you"* (v. 12). The call of God is never about our credentials; it's about His presence.

This passage reveals a powerful truth: God sees suffering, hears the cries of the oppressed, and acts through people—flawed, fearful people—who are willing to obey. God's plan for deliverance has always involved calling someone out of comfort into courageous faith.

We, like Moses, are often drawn to freedom's fire but scared of its cost. Yet God still speaks, still sends, and still promises to go with us. The injustice around us—whether in schools, communities, or systems—doesn't go unnoticed by heaven. The question is: Will we answer when God calls us to step in?

Personal Prayer:

> Lord, thank You for seeing the cries of the hurting and for calling people to bring Your justice. Help me not to shrink from the calling on my life. Give me courage to go where You send, speak truth when it's hard, and trust that You go with me. In Jesus' name, Amen.

Prayer for the Nation:

God of justice and mercy, thank You for the freedom we enjoy. As You called Moses to confront oppression, call us to stand for truth in our nation. Raise up leaders with courage and compassion. Heal what is broken, protect the vulnerable, and help us be a people who seek righteousness, not just comfort. Go with us, Lord, as we pursue freedom not only for ourselves but for all. In Jesus' name, amen.

Memorable Quote:

"God's call isn't about who you are—it's about who goes with you."

Reflection:

1. What situation around you do you think breaks God's heart?
2. Where might God be calling you to act—even if it feels too big?
3. How can you grow your trust in God's presence rather than your own ability?

Day 4

No More Excuses

BiblePlan Reading: Exodus 4:1–17

Focus: Moses doubted himself, but God promised to equip him. God uses the willing, not the perfect.

Ponder: What excuses are holding you back from God's call?

Key Verse(s): *"Then the Lord said to him, 'Who has made man's mouth? Who makes him mute, or deaf, or seeing, or blind? Is it not I, the Lord?'"* — Exodus 4:11 (ESV)

When God called Moses to confront Pharaoh and lead Israel out of slavery, Moses didn't jump up with courage—he froze with insecurity. "What if they don't believe me?" "I'm not a good speaker." "Please send someone else." Sound familiar?

Moses had every excuse ready, and most of them were rooted in fear: fear of failure, fear of rejection, fear of inadequacy. But God wasn't looking for perfection—He was looking for willingness. God answered each of Moses' objections with reassurance: miraculous signs, divine authority, and finally, a partner in Aaron. Yet even as God patiently responded, there was a moment of anger—because God knew Moses was missing the point: *It was never about Moses' ability; it was about God's presence.*

When we feel called to speak up, step out, or stand firm for truth in a broken world, insecurity can silence us. But God is still asking, *"Who made your mouth?"* If He gave you a voice, He will give you the words. If He gave you a burden, He will give you the strength. The freedom fighters of faith are rarely the loudest or the strongest—they're simply the ones who say "yes" when God calls.

Don't let fear dress up as humility. God's not looking for someone who feels ready. He's looking for someone who is available. He'll take care of the rest.

PERSONAL PRAYER:

> Lord, You know every fear and weakness I carry. Thank You for Your patience when I make excuses. Teach me to trust Your power more than my limitations. I surrender my insecurities—use me however You choose to bring freedom, truth, and hope to the world around me. In Jesus' name, Amen.

Prayer for the Nation:

God of purpose and promise, we lift up our nation to You. So often, we as a people are held back by fear, division, and excuses that prevent us from pursuing what is right and just. Raise up leaders and citizens who, like Moses, may feel inadequate—but are willing. Remind us that our limitations are not the end, but the beginning of Your work through us. Give us courage to confront injustice, humility to rely on Your strength, and faith to move forward even when we feel unqualified. Equip this generation to speak truth, defend the vulnerable, and walk boldly in Your calling. Amen.

Memorable Quote:

"God doesn't call the qualified—He equips the willing."

Reflection:

1. What excuses have you been using to avoid God's call on your life?
2. How might your insecurities actually become opportunities for God to show His power?
3. Take one small step today in the direction of what you know God is asking you to do.

Day 5

When Courage Meets Resistance

BiblePlan Reading: Exodus 5:1–23

Focus: Obedience to God doesn't guarantee instant results. Moses faced resistance but stayed the course.

Ponder: How do you respond when obedience brings setbacks?

Key Verse(s): *"But Pharaoh said, 'Who is the Lord, that I should obey his voice and let Israel go? I do not know the Lord, and moreover, I will not let Israel go.'"—Exodus 5:2 (ESV)*

After finally surrendering to God's call, Moses steps into Pharaoh's courts with confidence. He delivers God's command with boldness: "Let my people go." But instead of surrender, Pharaoh responds with scorn. Rather than freedom, the Israelites get more oppression. Their workload increases, and their hope fades. And Moses? He questions everything. "Why did You ever send me?" (v. 22)

This moment reveals something deeply real about walking in obedience: doing the right thing doesn't always produce immediate victory. Sometimes, obedience leads first to rejection, confusion, or even backlash. God had called Moses to confront injustice—but the path to justice was not instant. It was filled with setbacks that tested his faith and refined his trust.

God's plan didn't fail. It was unfolding.

This story reminds us that spiritual freedom, like political freedom, often comes at a cost. Truth-tellers and freedom fighters must be willing to face resistance. Standing up to Pharaoh—whether it's a system, a lie, or a personal fear—requires courage that outlasts disappointment. Moses' boldness didn't change Pharaoh overnight, but it placed him firmly in God's will. And that's where breakthrough begins.

If obedience has led you into hardship instead of results, don't quit. Delayed outcomes don't mean divine absence. God is still working behind the scenes, shaping the outcome—and shaping you.

Personal Prayer:

> Lord, help me to obey Your call even when the path is hard and the results are delayed. Strengthen my courage when I face resistance, and remind me that You are working even when I can't see it. Teach me to trust Your timing and stand firm for truth and justice. In Jesus' name, Amen.

Prayer for the Nation:

God of justice and mercy, we pray for our nation today. Strengthen leaders and citizens who stand for freedom and righteousness. Help us to face opposition with courage and humility, and guide us toward lasting peace and justice. May Your Spirit empower us to be true freedom fighters in our communities. Amen.

Memorable Quote:

"Delayed results don't mean God's plan has failed—they mean His plan is still unfolding."

Reflection:

1. How do you typically respond when obedience leads to more pressure instead of less?
2. Is there a "Pharaoh" in your life you need to confront with truth and faith?
3. What would it look like to trust God's timing even when resistance seems stronger than results?

Day 6

The Power Behind the Mission

BiblePlan Reading: Exodus 7:1–13, 10:1–20

Focus: God alone breaks chains. Moses is bold, but it's God's power that delivers.

Ponder: Where do you need to trust God's power more than your own?

Key Verse(s): *"But I will harden Pharaoh's heart, and though I multiply my signs and wonders in the land of Egypt, Pharaoh will not listen to you. Then I will lay my hand on Egypt and bring my hosts, my people the children of Israel, out of the land of Egypt by great acts of judgment."*—Exodus 7:3–4 (ESV)

Moses stood before the most powerful man in the world with nothing but a staff and a promise. But that was enough—because the power wasn't in the staff or in Moses. It was in the God who sent him.

The showdown between Moses and Pharaoh wasn't a test of personalities—it was a revelation of power. Pharaoh represented oppressive human authority; God displayed divine justice. As plague after plague struck the land, Egypt's gods were mocked, and Pharaoh's heart was exposed. But it was never Moses' strength that turned the tide. It was the unstoppable hand of God moving through signs, wonders, and mercy withheld no longer.

Sometimes we think courage means having it all together. But Moses shows us that true courage is trusting in the One who *does*. Even when Pharaoh refused to budge, even when it seemed the mission was failing, God was in control—displaying His power not only to set Israel free, but to show that no oppressor, no injustice, no hardened heart can outlast His will.

We live in a world that needs deliverance—from spiritual bondage, injustice, and lies that enslave hearts. And like Moses, we are called to speak truth and stand firm. But we must remember: victory doesn't depend on our brilliance or strength. It depends on God. You are not the source of freedom—you're a vessel through which God reveals it.

Personal Prayer:

> Lord, I confess how often I try to carry the mission in my own strength. Remind me that You are the power behind every victory. Help me trust You fully when the task is overwhelming and the opposition fierce. Use me as a bold witness for Your truth and freedom. In Jesus' name, amen.

Freedom Fighters: Heroes of Faith Who Stood for Truth

PRAYER FOR THE NATION:

Father, we lift up our nation before You now. Just as You showed Your power to break the chains of Egypt, we pray You would break every chain of injustice, pride, and hardness of heart in our land. May Your mighty hand move to bring true freedom—freedom that only comes through You. Empower leaders and citizens alike to rely not on their own strength but on Your sovereign power. Raise up deliverers who trust in Your power to transform and restore. Let Your justice roll like a mighty river and Your truth be the foundation on which our nation stands. In Jesus' name, amen.

MEMORABLE QUOTE:

"God doesn't need your strength—just your surrender."

REFLECTION:

1. Where are you trying to force results instead of trusting God's timing and power?
2. How does remembering God's power give you courage in the face of resistance?
3. Ask God today to show you where He wants to demonstrate His power through your obedience.

Day 7

Freedom Walks Forward

BiblePlan Reading: Exodus 12:21–42 & Exodus 14:1–31

Focus: The Passover and the Red Sea miracle marked Israel's physical freedom—and a new walk with God.

Ponder: Are you living like someone God has already set free?

Key Verse(s): *"The Lord will fight for you, and you have only to be silent."*—Exodus 14:14 (ESV)

After centuries of slavery, one final night changed everything. The blood of a lamb on their doors spared the Israelites from death. The next morning, they walked out of Egypt—not as captives, but as a people redeemed by the mighty hand of God. But freedom wasn't just about leaving Egypt—it was about learning to trust the God who leads, even when the way forward seems impossible.

As Pharaoh's army pursued them to the edge of the Red Sea, panic set in. Had they come all this way only to die in the desert? But God wasn't finished showing them what freedom looked like. He told them to stand still—not to run, not to fight, not to beg—just to trust. And then He made a way where there was no way. The sea split. The people walked forward. The oppressors drowned. God didn't just deliver them—He destroyed the enemy behind them.

Freedom in Christ works the same way. Jesus, our Passover Lamb, shed His blood to set us free from sin and death. But freedom isn't just about escaping the past—it's about trusting God with every step forward. Spiritual freedom means we no longer live enslaved to fear, shame, or sin. We follow the One who fights for us.

So the question isn't just, "Has God set you free?"—but *"Are you walking like someone who is?"* The true fight for freedom has already been won. Now it's time to walk forward in faith.

PERSONAL PRAYER:

> God, thank You for fighting my battles and setting me free through Christ. Help me walk forward in faith, not fear—trusting that You still make a way where there seems to be none. Let my life be a testimony to Your power and grace. In Jesus' name, amen.

PRAYER FOR THE NATION:

> Lord, we pray for our nation today. May we not forget the source of true freedom—You. Raise up leaders of justice, humility, and courage. Heal our divisions, protect the oppressed, and lead our people to walk in righteousness and truth. Let Your grace shape the soul of our land.

MEMORABLE QUOTE:

"Freedom isn't just about what God brings you out of—it's about who you trust as you walk forward."

REFLECTION:

1. Are there places in your life where you're still living like a slave instead of someone set free?
2. What fears or past chains do you need to leave behind at the edge of the Red Sea?
3. How can you live boldly today as someone God has already delivered?

Part 2

ESTHER: COURAGE IN THE SHADOWS

An 8-Day Journey of Courage, Calling, and God's Hidden Hand

Even when God seems silent, He's working behind the scenes. Discover how Esther's bold faith and strategic obedience turned the tide for a nation—and how God may be calling you for "such a time as this."

Memory Verse:
"Who knows but that you have come to your royal position for such a time as this?"
—Esther 4:14

Day 8

God's Hand in Hidden Places

BiblePlan Reading: Esther 1:1–22

Focus: God's name isn't mentioned in the book of Esther—but His fingerprints are everywhere. Even Vashti's refusal was part of God's setup.

Ponder: Where might God be working behind the scenes in your life?

Key Verse(s): *"But Queen Vashti refused to come at the king's command delivered by the eunuchs. Then the king became furious and burned with anger."*—Esther 1:12 (ESV)

The book of Esther begins in a palace filled with pomp, power, and pride. King Xerxes rules over a vast empire, and Queen Vashti is summoned to display her beauty before drunken nobles. She refuses—an act of defiance that shocks the kingdom and results in her removal. It looks like a royal scandal, not a holy moment. And yet, it's the first domino in a divine plan.

Interestingly, the name of God is never mentioned in the book of Esther. Not once. But that doesn't mean He's absent. His hand is present in every twist and turn—from Vashti's refusal, to Esther's rise, to the salvation of an entire people. God works in the quiet shadows, weaving justice and deliverance through the most unlikely events and people.

When we fight for truth and freedom today, we often long for visible signs that God is with us. But sometimes, God chooses to stay hidden—His work disguised in detours, delays, and even disappointments. Vashti's bold "no" wasn't just personal courage—it became a divine setup for Esther's entrance and Israel's preservation.

If you're in a season where God feels silent or unseen, take heart: He is not absent. He may be preparing something greater than you can imagine. Freedom sometimes begins with a disruption. Justice often unfolds through quiet resistance. Truth can be set in motion by a single act of courage—seen or unseen.

Personal Prayer:

> Lord, when I cannot see Your hand, help me trust Your heart. Give me faith to believe that You are working even in the hidden places of my life. Let me be willing to stand firm, even when I don't understand the outcome.

PRAYER FOR THE NATION:

> Father, thank You for being the God who works in hidden ways. We ask that You guide our nation with unseen wisdom and justice. Raise up leaders who will stand for truth, and use even unexpected events to bring about Your redemptive purposes.

MEMORABLE QUOTE:

"God's name may be hidden in the shadows, but His fingerprints are always on the story."

REFLECTION:

1. Can you think of a time when something that seemed disappointing later revealed God's purpose?
2. Where in your life do you sense God might be working behind the scenes right now?
3. What small act of courage can you take today, trusting God to use it for a greater purpose?

Day 9

Positioned with a Purpose

BiblePlan Reading: Esther 2:1–18

Focus: Esther wasn't just beautiful—she was chosen. God positioned her in the palace for more than comfort.

Ponder: What places or roles has God given you that might serve a higher purpose?

Key Verse(s): *"Now the king was attracted to Esther more than to any of the other women, and she won his favor and approval more than any of the other virgins. So he set a royal crown on her head and made her queen instead of Vashti."*—Esther 2:17

Esther's rise to royalty wasn't just the result of her outer beauty—it was the unfolding of divine strategy. Hidden behind palace walls and political protocol, God was moving pieces into place. Esther might have seemed like just another young woman swept into a king's harem, but heaven saw her as a key player in a rescue plan for God's people.

Though the name of God is never mentioned in the book of Esther, His fingerprints are unmistakable. From the removal of Queen Vashti to Esther's selection as queen, we see God positioning people and circumstances to fulfill His purposes. Esther's beauty may have opened doors, but her calling required courage. She was not placed in the palace for her own comfort—she was placed there for such a time as this.

In our world today, it's tempting to view our careers, relationships, or platforms as ends in themselves. But what if they're actually part of something bigger? What if God has placed you right where you are—your job, your classroom, your community—not just for your benefit, but to be a voice for truth and an advocate for justice?

Just as Esther was positioned to stand in the gap for her people, we too are called to use our influence—however great or small—to serve others and honor God. Spiritual freedom often begins with one person saying "yes" to a divine assignment they didn't expect but were prepared to fulfill.

Personal Prayer:

> Lord, help me to see that I am not where I am by accident. Open my eyes to the ways You are calling me to stand for truth and serve with courage. May I live with purpose, even in the unseen places.

Prayer for the Nation:

God of justice and mercy, raise up leaders and everyday heroes in our nation who will courageously use their positions to defend the vulnerable, uphold truth, and promote freedom. Position our country to reflect Your heart for righteousness and peace.

Memorable Quote

"God doesn't just place us—He positions us for purpose."

Reflection

1. Where has God placed you right now that may be part of a bigger plan?
2. How can you use your influence, no matter how small it seems, to speak truth or serve others?
3. Ask God today: "What is Your purpose for me in this place?"

Day 10

When Evil Has a Platform

BiblePlan Reading: Esther 3:1–15

Focus: Haman's hatred reveals how evil can rise—but God is not absent. Esther's people are under threat, but hope isn't lost.

Ponder: How do you respond when injustice seems to win?

Key Verse(s): *"Then the king's secretaries were summoned on the thirteenth day of the first month, and an edict...was written in the name of King Xerxes and sealed with his own ring."*—Esther 3:12, NIV

When Haman was promoted, it seemed like evil had won the microphone. Fueled by pride and prejudice, Haman's hatred for Mordecai quickly expanded into a genocidal plan targeting all the Jewish people. With the king's signet ring in his grasp, Haman didn't just gain influence—he gained power. And he used it to elevate a lie: that God's people were a threat to the kingdom.

At this moment in the story, God's name is not mentioned. No miracles, no burning bush, no angelic rescue. Just an unrelenting decree of death. But this is where the story gets real—and familiar. Because sometimes it *does* feel like evil gets the stage, the power, and the last word. Sometimes it feels like truth is silenced, and the righteous are overrun.

But the God of Esther is never absent. He is the hidden hand moving behind the curtain of circumstances, preparing a courageous response, aligning people in the right place at the right time. Just because evil has a platform doesn't mean God has left the room.

As followers of Christ, we are called to stand when truth is twisted and freedom is threatened. Not with hatred or panic—but with courage, prayer, and wisdom. Esther's story reminds us: evil may rise, but it will not reign. God is still working, even in the silence.

Personal Prayer:

> Lord, when injustice seems loud and evil gains ground, remind me that You are not absent. Give me courage to stand for truth even when it costs something. Let my hope be rooted in Your sovereignty.

PRAYER FOR THE NATION:

> God of justice, we lift up our nation. When evil seems to find a platform, raise up leaders of integrity and voices of truth. Protect the vulnerable, expose deception, and bring righteousness to the forefront once again.

MEMORABLE QUOTE:

"Evil may rise, but it will not reign—God is still working, even in the silence."

REFLECTION:

1. How do you usually respond when injustice seems to win? Panic, silence, prayer, action?
2. Where do you see "Haman-like" influence in your world today, and how can you stand with courage and truth in that place?
3. Take time to pray for someone suffering under injustice today—name them and ask God to intervene.

Day 11

For Such a Time as This

BiblePlan Reading: Esther 4:1–17

Focus: Mordecai challenges Esther to act, not hide. Her fear is real—but so is her calling.

Ponder: What fears do you need to surrender to follow God's purpose for you?

Key Verse(s): *"And who knows but that you have come to your royal position for such a time as this?"*—Esther 4:14 (NIV)

When Esther first hears of Mordecai's mourning, she is sheltered behind palace walls—safe, for the moment, from the death sentence hanging over her people. But safety isn't the same as purpose. Mordecai sends her a message that cuts to the heart: Don't think you can escape. Don't think silence will save you. *You were made for this.*

Esther's fear was real. Approaching the king uninvited was punishable by death. But Mordecai's words reframed her fear into faith: perhaps God placed her there *not* to be safe, but to be *significant*. The call wasn't to be fearless, but to be faithful.

In a world where truth is often silenced and justice distorted, courage means more than bold speeches—it means quiet decisions to risk comfort for conviction. Like Esther, we are not where we are by accident. Your job, your school, your community—it's no mistake. You, too, may be placed "for such a time as this."

This story also reminds us of God's hidden hand. His name is never mentioned in the book of Esther, yet His fingerprints are on every page. He is working behind the scenes—even when we're unsure, even when we're afraid.

Today, what fear is holding you back? Is it the fear of rejection, failure, or losing security? Like Esther, you are invited to surrender that fear to a greater purpose—to stand for truth, freedom, and the gospel of justice.

PERSONAL PRAYER:

> Lord, I confess the fears that keep me silent and hesitant. Give me courage to step into the calling You've placed on my life. Help me trust that You are with me, even when I can't see the way forward. Amen.

Prayer for the Nation:

> God of justice and truth, raise up leaders and citizens alike who will stand with courage for what is right. Awaken our nation to its divine calling—not just to prosper, but to protect the vulnerable and uphold freedom for all. May we not shrink back, but rise up for such a time as this. In Jesus' Name, Amen.

Memorable Quote:

"God doesn't call us to be fearless—He calls us to be faithful in the face of fear."

Reflection:

1. What fear might God be calling you to surrender today?
2. Where has He placed you "for such a time as this"?
3. This week, speak truth or act justly in one specific situation—especially if it costs you something.

Day 12

The Power of a Pause

BiblePlan Reading: Esther 5:1–8

Focus: Esther doesn't rush. She approaches the king with both courage and strategy. Faith isn't reckless—it's wise and Spirit-led.

Ponder: Are you trusting God's timing, or pushing your own?

Key Verse(s): *"If I have found favor in the sight of the king, and if it pleases the king to grant my petition and fulfill my request, let the king and Haman come to the banquet which I will prepare for them, and tomorrow I will do as the king has said."*—Esther 5:8 (NKJV)

Esther's life was on the line. The moment she stepped into the king's court without being summoned, she risked death. And yet, her first move after being received wasn't a fiery speech or a dramatic reveal of Haman's plot. Instead, she invited the king to a banquet—not once, but twice. Esther had already shown courage by stepping into the court, but here we see a different kind of courage: wisdom wrapped in patience.

In a world that often demands immediate action, Esther teaches us the value of strategic faith. She knew when to speak and when to wait. She trusted not only God's calling, but His timing. Her pause wasn't cowardice; it was discernment. Esther sensed that hearts weren't ready yet, and she had the humility to wait for God's hand to move.

God isn't just interested in the bold *what*—He's invested in the faithful *how* and *when*. As freedom fighters for truth and justice, we must learn to speak boldly while walking wisely. Boldness isn't recklessness. It's being led by the Spirit, not driven by fear or impulse.

Are you trying to force something ahead of God's timing? Esther reminds us: trust God's strategy. His wisdom often comes in whispers and waits. Her story assures us that even in silence, God is working.

Personal Prayer:

> Lord, give me the courage to act and the wisdom to wait. Teach me to follow Your lead instead of rushing ahead. Help me discern the moments to speak and the moments to be still. I trust Your timing more than my own urgency. Amen.

PRAYER FOR THE NATION:

> God, raise up leaders in our land who walk in both boldness and wisdom. Let justice be pursued not only with strength, but with discernment. Teach our nation to trust in Your timing and follow Your ways, even when patience is required. Amen.

MEMORABLE QUOTE:

"Faith doesn't rush the moment—it trusts the Master."

REFLECTION:

1. Are you rushing into action without waiting on God's direction?
2. Where might God be asking you to slow down and trust His timing?
3. What would it look like to combine bold courage with Holy Spirit wisdom in your current situation?

Day 13

Flip the Script

BiblePlan Reading: Esther 6:1–14

Focus: The king can't sleep—and divine irony unfolds. God flips the script for His glory.

Ponder: Have you ever seen God turn the enemy's plan on its head?

Key Verse(s): *"That night the king could not sleep. So he gave orders to bring the book of the chronicles, the record of his reign, and it was found written that Mordecai had exposed Bigthana and Teresh, two of the king's officers who guarded the doorway, who had conspired to assassinate King Xerxes."*—Esther 6:1 (NIV)

Have you ever witnessed a moment so packed with divine irony that it could only be orchestrated by God Himself? Esther 6 delivers one of those unforgettable turnarounds. The night before Haman plans to ask for Mordecai's execution, King Xerxes has a case of royal insomnia. But this is no coincidence—it's providence.

In what can only be described as God's hidden hand at work, the king "randomly" discovers Mordecai's long-forgotten act of loyalty. Instead of condemning Mordecai, the king honors him. Even more dramatically, it is Haman—Mordecai's enemy—who is commanded to lead the parade, praising the very man he planned to destroy. The irony is not lost. God's justice, though sometimes delayed, is never denied.

This moment in Esther's story is a powerful reminder that God is not passive. When we stand for truth, even in the shadows, God is working behind the scenes. He flips scripts. He reverses outcomes. He brings down pride and lifts up the humble. And when He moves, it's unmistakable.

In our own battles—whether for spiritual freedom, justice, or truth—we may not always see immediate results. But like Mordecai, we can trust the Author of history to remember, redeem, and reverse. No enemy plan can outmaneuver the will of God.

PERSONAL PRAYER:

> Lord, thank You for being the God who sees and acts in perfect timing. When I feel forgotten or unseen, remind me of Your sovereignty. Help me to trust Your hidden hand and stand for truth even when I can't see the outcome. Amen.

PRAYER FOR THE NATION:

God of justice, awaken our nation to Your truth. Reverse the plans of the enemy, expose what's hidden, and raise up leaders who walk in humility and righteousness. May Your glory be seen in every reversal. In Jesus' Name, Amen.

MEMORABLE QUOTE:

"God doesn't just write the story—He rewrites what the enemy meant for harm into a display of His glory."

REFLECTION:

1. Where have you seen God "flip the script" in your life or the life of someone else?
2. What would it look like for you to trust God's timing when you're waiting for justice?
3. This week, choose one way to stand for truth even when it's not immediately rewarded.

Day 14

Justice Comes

BiblePlan Reading: Esther 7:1–10

Focus: Esther speaks up. Haman falls. Courage leads to breakthrough—but not without risk.

Ponder: What situation in your life needs bold truth spoken in love?

Key Verse(s): *"So they hanged Haman on the gallows that he had prepared for Mordecai. Then the king's wrath subsided."*—Esther 7:10 (NKJV)

The king, the queen, and the villain sit at one final banquet. Esther knows this is the moment everything turns—or everything falls apart. She takes a breath and does the unthinkable: she names Haman as the enemy, the one who schemed to destroy her people. The king is shocked. Haman panics. And in a divine reversal, the trap he laid for Mordecai becomes his own undoing.

Esther's courage breaks the silence. Her risk uncovers truth. And justice rolls in like a flood.

This passage doesn't just highlight a climactic moment in a royal palace—it unveils the deeper truth of God's justice. The God of Esther is not silent. Even when His name is hidden in the text, His hand is at work, exposing evil, honoring faithfulness, and defending the oppressed. Justice, in God's timing, is not always immediate, but it is always sure.

Esther's boldness is a challenge to us. Speaking truth can cost us comfort, reputation, or even safety—but truth, spoken in love and wisdom, can shake thrones and shift history. Whether it's confronting injustice, defending the vulnerable, or calling out wrongdoing with grace, God calls His people to be voices of truth in a world of shadows.

Justice came to Persia that day because one woman stood with courage. What might happen in our homes, communities, or nation if we did the same?

PERSONAL PRAYER:

> Lord, give me the courage to speak truth with grace, even when it costs me something. Help me trust Your justice, even when I cannot yet see it. Use my voice to stand for what is right.

Prayer for the Nation:

God of justice, raise up leaders and citizens who will speak truth, defend the innocent, and pursue what is right. Let righteousness and mercy guide our land. Let courage silence corruption, and may Your justice be done in our nation.

Memorable Quote:

"When courage finds its voice, justice begins to speak."

Reflection:

1. Where in your life is God calling you to speak the truth in love?
2. Is there an injustice or situation you've stayed silent about? What would courage look like there?
3. Ask God today to reveal one step of obedience you can take toward being a voice for truth.

Day 15

From Surviving to Thriving

BiblePlan Reading: Esther 8:1–17

Focus: Esther doesn't stop at survival—she secures freedom for her people. Her obedience leads to celebration.

Ponder: How might God use your courage to bless others?

Key Verse(s): *"For the Jews it was a time of happiness and joy, gladness and honor."*—Esther 8:16 (NIV)

Esther didn't just seek protection for herself—she used her position to bring deliverance and dignity to her people. In Esther 8, we witness a powerful shift. The threat of annihilation is reversed. Mordecai is elevated. Esther's influence at the palace becomes a catalyst for national liberation. What began as quiet courage in the shadows has now become public justice in the light.

God's name is never mentioned in the book of Esther, yet His providential hand is unmistakable. Through Esther's bold advocacy, God orchestrates freedom. What was meant for destruction becomes a reason for joy. The Jews move from weeping to celebration, from fear to honor. Esther could have stopped after saving herself and Mordecai, but she didn't settle for survival—she fought for the flourishing of her people.

This is the heartbeat of biblical courage: it doesn't retreat after personal victory. True courage presses forward so that others can walk free too. God often uses one person's obedience to unlock freedom for many. Like Esther, we're called not just to endure, but to act—to stand, speak, and serve in a way that brings justice, dignity, and hope to those around us.

In a world that still battles fear, injustice, and oppression, your courage matters. Your stand for truth—whether in your school, workplace, community, or home—can spark a ripple of freedom for others. You might not wear a crown, but you carry Christ. And He has placed you where you are "for such a time as this."

PERSONAL PRAYER:

> Lord, thank You for the courage of Esther and the freedom You gave her people. Help me to use the influence You've given me not just for myself, but for the good of others. Give

me boldness to stand for truth and to bless those in need of hope. Amen.

PRAYER FOR THE NATION:

Father, we pray for our nation—that justice would roll like a river and righteousness like a never-failing stream. Raise up leaders and citizens who will not just seek survival but the thriving of all people. May we be a land where truth and freedom flourish under Your guidance. Amen.

MEMORABLE QUOTE:

"Courage doesn't stop at survival—it carries others into freedom."

REFLECTION:

1. Is there a "next step" God is calling you to take that goes beyond your own comfort?
2. How can you use your voice or position to bring freedom or hope to someone else this week?
3. Celebrate with someone who has experienced a breakthrough—joy is part of the testimony.

Part 3

DANIEL: STANDING TALL IN A FALLEN WORLD

A 9-Day Journey on Courage, Conviction, and God's Sovereignty

---

Daniel lived in a culture that didn't honor God—but he never wavered in his devotion. This plan will help you explore how to stay faithful to your beliefs, stand with integrity, and trust God in hostile or compromising environments.

Memory Verse:
"The people who know their God shall stand firm and take action."
—Daniel 11:32b (ESV)

Day 16

Exiled, Not Forsaken

BiblePlan Reading: Daniel 1:1–7

Focus: Daniel is taken from his homeland, but God's presence goes with him. Even in exile, God is in control.

Ponder: How do you respond when you're pulled out of your comfort zone?

Key Verse(s): *"And the Lord gave Jehoiakim king of Judah into his hand, with some of the vessels of the house of God…"*—Daniel 1:2a (ESV)

Being ripped from your home, your culture, and your people is more than a crisis of place—it's a crisis of identity. When Babylon conquered Jerusalem, Daniel and his friends were among the brightest young men taken into exile, absorbed into a pagan empire. On the surface, it seemed like defeat. God's temple was raided. His people were scattered. And Daniel was given a new name, a new language, and a new life far from the land he called home.

But the story doesn't end with Babylon's power. In fact, the passage subtly reminds us that God was still in control. *"The Lord gave Jehoiakim king of Judah into his hand..."* (v.2). God allowed this. He wasn't absent in the exile—He was actively present, even orchestrating the events for His greater purpose.

This is the heartbeat of the book of Daniel: though kingdoms rise and fall, God remains sovereign. Daniel may have lost everything familiar, but he hadn't lost God's presence. In exile, he would discover deeper faith, develop courageous conviction, and become a vessel through whom God would speak to kings.

When we're pulled from our comfort zones—through tragedy, transition, or trial—it can feel like exile. But just like Daniel, we are exiled, not forsaken. The same God who was with Daniel in Babylon walks with us in our hardest moments. He is not confined to a land, a temple, or a time period. He is with His people, wherever they are.

In this cultural moment, standing for truth, freedom, and justice may take us into unfamiliar, uncomfortable territory. But we don't stand alone. God's presence goes before us, and His sovereignty stands above every earthly power.

Personal Prayer:

> Lord, when life pulls me out of the familiar, remind me that I'm never out of Your reach. Give me courage like Daniel to

trust You when I feel lost. You are with me, even in exile. Amen.

Prayer for the Nation:

Father, in times when our nation seems to drift from truth, may we not lose heart. Raise up men and women of conviction. Remind us that You are sovereign over every government and every moment in history. Be near to us in seasons of uncertainty.

Memorable Quote:

"Exile may change your surroundings, but it can't cancel God's presence or purpose in your life."

Reflection:

1. Where do you feel "exiled" or outside your comfort zone right now?
2. How can you trust God's presence even when your surroundings change?
3. This week, look for one way to be a faithful witness, even in an unfamiliar or uncomfortable place.

Day 17

Conviction Over Compromise

BiblePlan Reading: Daniel 1:8–21

Focus: Daniel resolves not to defile himself. His quiet stand for God leads to unexpected favor.

Ponder: Where are you tempted to blend in instead of stand out for God?

Key Verse(s): *"But Daniel resolved not to defile himself with the royal food and wine, and he asked the chief official for permission not to defile himself this way."*—Daniel 1:8 (NIV)

When Babylon conquered Jerusalem, Daniel and his friends were stripped of their homes, names, and culture. Everything familiar was replaced with foreign customs—and a royal training program meant to mold them into Babylonian servants. Yet right in the middle of this re-education, Daniel quietly drew a line. He resolved not to defile himself with the king's food and wine, likely because it violated God's dietary laws or had been offered to idols.

Daniel didn't protest loudly or demand his rights. He simply made a humble request—and trusted God with the outcome. God honored Daniel's quiet courage, granting him favor with officials and blessing him with wisdom and strength. By the end of the trial period, Daniel and his friends stood out—not because they blended in, but because they stood firm.

In today's culture, the pressure to compromise biblical values is strong. Whether it's in the classroom, workplace, or even among friends, blending in often feels safer than standing out. But freedom doesn't come from fitting in—it comes from faithful obedience to God. Daniel's story reminds us that courage isn't always loud. Sometimes, it's a quiet resolve to live God's way, even when no one else does.

God is faithful to those who honor Him. He's not just watching our big moments—He's present in the small, everyday decisions we make to choose truth over comfort, purity over popularity, and conviction over compromise.

PERSONAL PRAYER:

> Lord, give me Daniel's courage to stand firm in my convictions, even when it's easier to blend in. Help me honor You in every decision—big or small—and trust You with the results. Strengthen me to live with quiet integrity. In Jesus' name, Amen.

Prayer for the Nation:

God, raise up Daniels in this generation—men and women who will stand for truth without compromise. Bless our nation with leaders and citizens who choose conviction over convenience. May we be a people who honor You above all else. Amen.

Memorable Quote:

"Conviction doesn't always shout—it often whispers, 'I will not defile myself.'"

Reflection:

1. Where are you tempted to go along with the crowd instead of standing firm in your faith?
2. What small decision can you make today to honor God, even if no one else notices?

Day 18

The God Who Knows All

BiblePlan Reading: Daniel 2:1–30

Focus: When the king demands the impossible, Daniel seeks God. True wisdom comes from above.

Ponder: Do you bring impossible situations to God in prayer—or try to figure them out yourself?

Key Verse(s): *"But there is a God in heaven who reveals mysteries…"*—Daniel 2:28a (ESV)

Nebuchadnezzar had everything—power, armies, riches. But one troubling dream stripped him of peace. Not only did he demand an interpretation, but he insisted that his advisors first tell him what the dream *was*, or die trying. It was a humanly impossible task. No one, they argued, could do this—except the gods, "whose dwelling is not with flesh" (v.11). They were half right. The answer wouldn't come from earthly wisdom, but from the One true God—who *does* dwell with His people.

Daniel didn't panic. He didn't scheme. He gathered his friends, and they prayed. When God revealed the mystery, Daniel didn't take credit. He gave all glory to the "God in heaven who reveals mysteries." Daniel's bold faith wasn't about knowing all the answers—it was about knowing *the One who does.*

This story reminds us that spiritual courage doesn't mean we always have a plan. Sometimes, the bravest thing we can do is admit we don't—and ask God to show up. We live in a world where truth is often blurred, where pressure mounts to conform, and where many problems seem unsolvable. But just like in Babylon, there is still a God in heaven. He still reveals truth. He still grants wisdom. And He still answers prayer.

When you face impossible decisions, injustice, or confusion, don't rely on your own understanding. Seek the God who sees what you can't. Stand tall, not in your knowledge, but in your trust in Him. God loves to reveal His truth through those humble enough to ask.

Personal Prayer:

> God of all wisdom, when life feels overwhelming, remind me that You know what I don't. Help me seek You first instead of trying to figure things out on my own. Reveal Your truth and guide me with clarity and courage. Amen.

Prayer for the Nation:

Lord, we ask that You raise up Daniels in our nation—people of integrity, prayer, and bold trust in You. In a time of confusion and division, reveal Your truth to our leaders and citizens. May we become a people who seek divine wisdom over human pride. Amen.

Memorable Quote:

"True courage isn't having all the answers—it's knowing the God who does."

Reflection:

1. When was the last time you faced an "impossible" situation? How did you respond?
2. Are you quick to seek God in prayer—or do you rely on your own problem-solving?
3. This week, make space for silence and prayer before making decisions. Ask God to reveal what you cannot see.

Day 19

The God Who Sees Tomorrow

BiblePlan Reading: Daniel 2:31–49

Focus: God shows Daniel a vision of future kingdoms. God alone holds history in His hands.

Ponder: How does God's control over the future give you peace in the present?

Key Verse(s): *"The great God has shown the king what will take place in the future. The dream is true, and its interpretation is trustworthy."*—Daniel 2:45b (NIV)

King Nebuchadnezzar had a troubling dream—one no magician, sorcerer, or wise man in Babylon could explain. That's when God stepped in. Through Daniel, a young exile who remained faithful in a foreign land, God revealed the king's vision of a great statue representing future empires—from Babylon to Rome—and ultimately, God's everlasting Kingdom.

Daniel didn't just interpret a dream—he revealed the nature of God Himself. This moment reminds us that history isn't random or ruled by the powerful. It is held in the hands of a sovereign God who sees tomorrow with perfect clarity. Kings rise and fall. Nations flourish and fade. But God's Kingdom will never be destroyed.

For Daniel, this wasn't just theology. It was courage-fueling truth. In a hostile culture, Daniel stood tall not because he knew the future, but because he knew the God who did. When the world feels chaotic and uncertain, we can stand for truth, freedom, and justice with that same confidence. God isn't guessing at what comes next—He's already there.

When we remember that God is in control of history, we're freed from fear. We don't need to compromise to survive or panic when truth feels threatened. Like Daniel, we can walk in bold obedience today because the future is already secure in the hands of our faithful God.

PERSONAL PRAYER:

> God, thank You that I don't have to fear the future. You are the One who sees it, shapes it, and reigns over it. Help me live with courage today, trusting that Your Kingdom will outlast every earthly power. Amen.

Prayer for the Nation:

> Lord, raise up leaders in our nation who will seek truth and justice, and remind us that no human kingdom will last forever. May we place our hope not in politics, but in You, the God who holds the future. Let Your Kingdom come. Amen.

Memorable Quote:

"God's control over the future gives us courage to stand for truth in the present."

Reflection:

1. In what ways are you tempted to fear the future, and how can you trust God instead?
2. How might remembering God's eternal Kingdom affect the way you live today?
3. What's one step you can take to stand for truth, knowing that God already holds tomorrow?

Day 20

Courage in the Fire

BiblePlan Reading: Daniel 3:1–30

Focus: Daniel's friends refuse to bow. God doesn't deliver them *from* the fire, but *in* it.

Ponder: Would you still trust God even if He didn't rescue you right away?

Key Verse(s): *"If we are thrown into the blazing furnace, the God we serve is able to deliver us from it… But even if he does not, we want you to know, Your Majesty, that we will not serve your gods or worship the image of gold you have set up."*—Daniel 3:17–18 (NIV)

Shadrach, Meshach, and Abednego stood in front of the most powerful king on earth—and said no. No to bowing. No to compromise. No to fear. They didn't shout or protest; they simply stood their ground. With one simple decision, they risked everything, knowing full well that their obedience to God could cost them their lives.

But their boldness wasn't rooted in certainty of rescue—it was grounded in trust. They believed God could save them. Yet their faith wasn't dependent on what God would do, but on who He is. *"But even if He does not..."* may be the most courageous words in all of Scripture.

God didn't keep them from the fire. He met them *in* it. A fourth figure—divine and glorious—appeared beside them in the flames. And when they stepped out, not a single hair was singed. No smoke. No burns. Just freedom.

This story reminds us that true spiritual freedom isn't the absence of trials—it's the presence of God in the middle of them. Like these three heroes, we are called to stand for truth, even when culture demands we bow. We may not face fiery furnaces, but we face peer pressure, ridicule, injustice, and fear. And just like them, we must decide: will we trust God when the heat is on?

God honors those who stand for Him. And even when deliverance doesn't come right away, His presence is always with us.

PERSONAL PRAYER:

> Lord, help me to stand firm when it's hard to follow You. Strengthen my heart when the heat rises. Teach me to trust You, not just when You rescue, but even when You don't—yet. Walk with me through every fire. Amen.

Prayer for the Nation:

Father, raise up a generation in this nation who won't bow to lies, injustice, or compromise. Give our leaders courage, our churches conviction, and our people faith that holds fast in the fire. Be near to us, Lord—especially when we walk through flames. Amen.

Memorable Quote:

"God may not always deliver us from the fire, but He will always meet us in it."

Reflection:

1. Would you still obey God if it meant facing loss or persecution?
2. What "fire" are you walking through right now where you need to trust God's presence over His immediate deliverance?
3. How can you stand for truth and freedom with courage this week?

Day 21

The Courage to Speak, the Grace to Bow

BiblePlan Reading: Daniel 4:1–37

Focus: Daniel lovingly confronts King Nebuchadnezzar. Truth and humility go hand in hand.

Ponder: Do you speak truth even when it's uncomfortable?

Key Verse(s): *"The decision is announced by messengers, the holy ones declare the verdict, so that the living may know that the Most High is sovereign over all kingdoms on earth and gives them to anyone he wishes and sets over them the lowliest of people."*—Daniel 4:17 (NIV)

Nebuchadnezzar was the most powerful man on earth—and the most prideful. But God, in His mercy, didn't destroy him. Instead, He gave him a warning. And Daniel, God's faithful servant, was the one tasked with delivering that hard truth.

When the king had a troubling dream, Daniel was terrified—not of the vision, but of how the king might respond. Yet he didn't shrink back. With respect and sorrow, Daniel told Nebuchadnezzar that his pride would lead to a humiliating fall, and that only repentance could save him from God's judgment.

This is humility in action. Daniel didn't gloat or speak with smug superiority. He loved the truth—but he also loved the person he was speaking to. He longed for the king to turn back before it was too late.

A year passed. The king didn't listen. He stood on his rooftop, basking in his own greatness, and just like that—God humbled him. Nebuchadnezzar lost his throne, his sanity, and his pride. But even that was grace. After seven years of brokenness, he lifted his eyes to heaven, and everything changed. He praised God, not himself. He finally understood: *God is King, and freedom begins when we surrender to Him.*

In a world that celebrates pride and silences truth, we need Daniels—people bold enough to speak hard truths and humble enough to do it with grace. Standing for truth doesn't mean shouting others down. It means pointing them up—to the One who reigns with justice and restores with mercy.

PERSONAL PRAYER:

> Father, give me the courage to speak the truth in love, even when it's uncomfortable. Help me to reflect Your humility,

so that others may see You through my words and actions. Teach me to value truth over approval and grace over pride.

Prayer for the Nation:

Lord, give us grace in this nation that we may humble ourselves where we have become proud. Raise up leaders and citizens who will speak truth with wisdom and walk in humility before You. May we remember that real freedom comes not from power, but from surrender to Your righteous rule.

Memorable Quote:

"Truth spoken with humility becomes a doorway to grace."

Reflection:

1. Is there someone in your life who needs to hear a hard truth in love? What's stopping you?
2. How do you balance courage and humility when standing for what's right?
3. Ask God to show you any areas of pride in your own heart

Day 22

Day 22

The Writing on the Wall

BiblePlan Reading: Daniel 5:1–31

Focus: A new king mocks God and faces judgment. Daniel remains steady, even when others are arrogant.

Ponder: Are you willing to be bold for God when everyone else is living carelessly?

Key Verse(s): *"You have been weighed on the scales and found wanting."*—Daniel 5:27 (NIV)

King Belshazzar threw a wild party. Drunk with pride and wine, he mocked God by using the sacred temple cups stolen from Jerusalem. While he and his guests praised idols of gold and silver, a mysterious hand appeared and wrote on the wall. Fear gripped the king. None of his wise men could interpret the message—until Daniel was called.

Years had passed since Daniel's glory days in Nebuchadnezzar's court, but his reputation for wisdom and integrity remained. He didn't sugarcoat the truth. Boldly, Daniel told Belshazzar that his arrogance and disrespect toward God had brought his kingdom to an end. That very night, the prophecy came true. Babylon fell, and Belshazzar died.

This moment in Scripture is more than a dramatic tale—it's a powerful warning and a call to courage. In a world where many live like truth doesn't matter, Daniel stood firm. He wasn't swayed by popularity, position, or pressure. His allegiance was to God, not the crowd.

God's justice is sure. He sees beyond the surface and weighs every heart. While His patience is long, His judgment is real. For those who mock Him, consequences will come. But for those who stand for truth—like Daniel—there is strength, peace, and purpose even in the middle of chaos.

As we reflect on our own culture today, with its celebration of self and rejection of God, we are reminded: real freedom isn't found in doing whatever we want—it's found in honoring the One who made us. And like Daniel, we are called to be truth-speakers in a world that needs a wake-up call.

Personal Prayer:

God, give me the courage to speak truth even when it's unpopular. Help me not to chase comfort or applause but to stay faithful to You, no matter what others are doing. Keep my heart humble and my eyes fixed on You. Amen.

Prayer for the Nation:

Lord, we pray for our nation. We have turned to idols of success, power, and self. Wake us up, God. Raise up leaders like Daniel—courageous, truthful, and surrendered to You. Let justice roll and mercy flow. In Jesus' name, Amen.

Memorable Quote:

"Real freedom isn't found in doing whatever we want—it's found in honoring the One who made us."

Reflection:

1. Are you willing to speak truth even if it makes others uncomfortable?
2. In what ways can you honor God with your words and actions today?
3. What idols does our culture worship—and how can you live differently?

Day 23

Standing Strong When It Counts

BiblePlan Reading: Daniel 6:1–28

Focus: Daniel keeps praying, even when it becomes illegal. His faith is tested, and God shows up.

Ponder: What "lions" are you facing, and how can faith lead you through them?

Key Verse(s): *"My God sent his angel, and he shut the mouths of the lions. They have not hurt me, because I was found innocent in his sight."*—Daniel 6:22a (NIV)

Daniel had spent decades serving pagan kings with excellence and integrity. But when a new law was passed banning prayer to anyone except King Darius, Daniel didn't flinch. He didn't protest publicly, pick a fight, or panic—he simply went home, opened his window, and prayed, just like he always had. He chose faith over fear.

Daniel knew what it could cost him. He had seen the cruelty of the Babylonian and Persian empires. But his allegiance wasn't to a throne on earth—it was to the King of heaven. So even when the law turned against his faith, he stayed true to God.

And yes, the lions' den was real. Cold stone walls, sharp teeth, and hungry predators. But so was the God who could shut the mouths of lions. Daniel didn't escape the trial—he was thrown into it. Yet God didn't abandon him. In the place of fear and death, God sent His angel and delivered him.

This story reminds us that standing for truth and righteousness isn't always safe or popular—but it is worth it. Daniel's courage shines as a beacon of spiritual freedom. His life challenges us: When the pressure builds, when culture turns hostile, will we stand firm in faith?

In a world full of "lions"—social pressure, rejection, injustice, and fear—God still calls His people to pray, to trust, and to stand. He may not always take us *out* of the den, but He will always go *with* us into it.

PERSONAL PRAYER:

> God, give me the courage to choose faith over fear. Help me stand for truth even when it costs me something. I trust that You are with me in every battle and every lion's den. Strengthen my heart to remain faithful to You. Amen.

Prayer for the Nation:

Lord, raise up Daniels in our land—people who stand boldly for truth, justice, and righteousness. May our nation turn to You in humility and courage. Protect those who walk with integrity, and silence the lions that seek to devour truth. Amen.

Memorable Quote:

"Faith doesn't avoid the lions—it faces them, knowing God is greater than the danger."

Reflection:

1. What "lion's den" are you facing right now? How can you stay faithful like Daniel?
2. Are there areas in your life where you've been choosing comfort over conviction?
3. How can your prayer life be an act of courage in a culture of compromise?

Day 24

A Kingdom That Cannot Fall

BiblePlan Reading: Daniel 7:1–28

Focus: Daniel receives terrifying visions—but also hope. God's kingdom will reign forever.

Ponder: In chaos and confusion, are your eyes fixed on the eternal King?
Key Verse(s): *"But the holy people of the Most High will receive the kingdom and will possess it forever—yes, for ever and ever."*—Daniel 7:18 (NIV)

Daniel's later chapters (7–12) are filled with visions—some strange, some frightening, and all deeply significant. Daniel saw beasts rising from the sea, kings clashing for power, nations falling, and evil forces raging. Yet through the chaos, a consistent truth rang out: *God is in control, and His kingdom will reign forever.*

In Daniel 7, the vision of four terrifying beasts represents powerful earthly empires. They seem unstoppable—until "the Ancient of Days" takes His throne. Then the "Son of Man" comes with the clouds of heaven and is given eternal authority, glory, and sovereign power. This is a clear prophecy pointing to Jesus Christ, whose kingdom will never end.

For Daniel—and for us—these visions remind us that earthly kingdoms rise and fall, but God's kingdom is unshakable. In a world filled with political turmoil, injustice, and moral confusion, it's easy to feel overwhelmed. But like Daniel, we're called to stand firm with courage and conviction, keeping our eyes fixed on the eternal King.

Even when the world feels like it's spinning out of control, God is writing the final chapter. His justice will prevail. His truth will outlast every lie. His freedom will break every chain.

As believers—*citizens of heaven*—we live with our feet on the ground but our hope anchored in eternity. We don't shrink back in fear. We press forward in faith, standing for what is right, living in the light, and pointing others to the only King whose rule brings true peace and lasting freedom.

PERSONAL PRAYER:

> Father, thank You that no matter what chaos surrounds me, Your kingdom stands firm. Help me live with hope, courage, and a heart that trusts You fully. Give me eternal vision, even in today's trials. In Jesus' name, Amen.

PRAYER FOR THE NATION:

> Lord, we lift our nation to You. In the midst of division, confusion, and darkness, raise up people of faith who live by Your truth. May Your justice roll like a river and Your kingdom come on earth as it is in heaven. Amen.

MEMORABLE QUOTE:

"When everything shakes, God's kingdom still stands—and so can we."

REFLECTION:

1. Where do you see confusion or chaos in your world right now? How can you fix your eyes on the eternal King?
2. What does it mean to live as a citizen of God's kingdom while still being active in this world?
3. Ask God to give you a vision that sees beyond today's struggles and into His forever promises.

Part 4

PAUL: FAITH THAT CAN'T BE LOCKED DOWN

A 9-Day Journey of Boldness, Endurance, and the Gospel on the Move

Chains couldn't silence him. Prisons couldn't stop him. Pain didn't shake his joy. The apostle Paul's life shows us how to live boldly for Christ—even when life shuts us in. This devotional explores how Paul preached, suffered, and rejoiced, all while advancing the kingdom of God in chains.

Memory Verse:
"I am not ashamed of the gospel,
for it is the power of God for salvation…"
—Romans 1:16

Day 25

Arrested by Grace

BiblePlan Reading: Acts 9:1–22

Focus: Before Paul was imprisoned for the gospel, he was set free by it. His radical transformation reminds us that God can redeem any story.

Ponder: Have you let God turn your past into purpose?

Key Verse(s): *"But the Lord said to Ananias, 'Go! This man is my chosen instrument to proclaim my name to the Gentiles and their kings and to the people of Israel.'"*—Acts 9:15 (NIV)

Before Paul preached freedom in Christ, he was a man in chains—chains of hate, pride, and self-righteousness. Acts 9 begins with Saul breathing threats and violence against Christians. He wasn't just lost; he was leading the charge against truth. But then, on the road to Damascus, everything changed. One encounter with Jesus blinded him physically but opened his spiritual eyes. The same man who once tried to silence the gospel became its boldest voice.

This moment is more than Paul's conversion—it's a vivid picture of grace on the move. God didn't wait for Paul to clean himself up or figure things out. Jesus met him at his worst and called him to something greater. That's the beauty of the gospel: it's not just about saving us *from* something but *for* something. Paul was "arrested" by grace—stopped in his tracks, turned around, and sent out with new purpose.

This same grace is available to us. Your past—no matter how messy—doesn't disqualify you. In fact, it may be the very thing God uses to shape your mission. Like Paul, you've been set free to stand for truth, speak with boldness, and live for something bigger than yourself. As our nation celebrates liberty, let's not forget that the greatest freedom is found in Christ—a freedom no prison, law, or enemy can take away.

PERSONAL PRAYER:

> Jesus, thank You for meeting me in my brokenness and calling me into freedom. Help me never forget what You've done for me. Use my past for Your purpose, and give me boldness to live out Your truth, no matter the cost. Amen.

PRAYER FOR THE NATION:

> God of justice and mercy, thank You for the freedom we enjoy in this nation. But more than that, we thank You for

the freedom we have in Christ. Raise up leaders and citizens transformed by Your grace. May Your truth bring healing, redemption, and purpose across this land. Amen.

MEMORABLE QUOTE:

"Grace doesn't just erase your past—it rewrites your future with purpose."

REFLECTION:

1. What in your past do you need to surrender so God can use it for His glory?
2. How can you boldly live out your freedom in Christ in today's culture of compromise?
3. This week, look for someone who feels too far gone—and remind them: God's grace can still reach them.

Day 26

Unshakable Joy in the Chains

BiblePlan Reading: Acts 16:16–34

Focus: Beaten and jailed in Philippi, Paul and Silas worship in the dark. Their joy leads to a jailer's salvation.

Ponder: Can you still sing when you're in a place that feels like a prison?

Key Verse(s): *"About midnight Paul and Silas were praying and singing hymns to God, and the other prisoners were listening to them."*—Acts 16:25 (NIV)

Paul and Silas were not just wrongly accused—they were stripped, beaten, and thrown into the deepest cell with their feet in stocks. This wasn't just inconvenient or unfair; it was brutal and humiliating. Yet when the night grew darkest, they did something unexpected—they sang.

Their worship wasn't just noise in the night; it was a declaration of freedom in Christ that no prison could silence. And that sound of praise cracked open more than just prison doors—it cracked open a hardened jailer's heart. When the earth quaked and the chains fell off, Paul and Silas didn't run. Their faith had already made them free, and their boldness led the jailer and his entire household to salvation.

This passage shows us a stunning picture of God's redemptive power. He doesn't waste our suffering. He turns pain into platforms for the gospel. He turns locked cells into revival meetings. When we stand boldly for truth—even when it costs us our comfort—God shows up in ways we never expected.

In a world that often worships safety and convenience, this kind of boldness is countercultural. But it's exactly what Jesus modeled and what His followers are called to. Like Paul and Silas, we're invited to sing in our darkest places—not because we enjoy the trial, but because we trust the One who is greater than the trial. That kind of boldness shakes foundations.

Personal Prayer:

> Lord, give me the courage to praise You when life feels like a prison. When I'm tempted to give in to fear or despair, help me remember that true freedom isn't found in my circumstances but in You. Let my worship be louder than my worry.

Prayer for the Nation:

God, awaken bold faith in our nation. Raise up people who will worship and witness even in the face of hardship. May our land echo with songs of freedom—not just political, but spiritual—and may Your truth shake what needs to be shaken so many can be set free.

Memorable Quote:

"Chains can't stop a heart that's free in Christ—and worship can turn a prison into a place of revival."

Reflection:

1. When have you experienced a "prison moment" in life? What did your response reveal about your trust in God?
2. What would it look like to choose worship over worry the next time you face injustice, fear, or hardship?
3. This week, how can your boldness in faith inspire someone else to believe?

Day 27

The Mission Doesn't Pause

BiblePlan Reading: Philippians 1:12–21

Focus: Even in chains, Paul saw his suffering as a platform for the gospel. He lived with heaven in view.

Ponder: How can you use your current struggle to point others to Jesus?

Key Verse(s): *"Now I want you to know, brothers and sisters, that what has happened to me has actually served to advance the gospel."*—Philippians 1:12 (NIV)

Even behind prison bars, Paul didn't see himself as stuck—he saw himself as sent. Locked up in Rome for preaching the gospel, Paul could've been discouraged. Instead, he saw his suffering as a stage where the glory of Jesus could shine even brighter. The gospel wasn't chained just because he was.

In Philippians 1, Paul explains that his imprisonment gave him a whole new audience. Guards were hearing about Jesus. Other believers were gaining courage to speak up. And Paul? He had one driving purpose: *"For to me, to live is Christ and to die is gain."* (v. 21). He lived like a free man, even when surrounded by chains, because his heart belonged to a greater kingdom.

This reveals something powerful about God—He never wastes our pain. He turns obstacles into opportunities and setbacks into setups for His glory. God's redemptive plan doesn't hit pause when life gets hard. In fact, some of the most powerful gospel moments are born from suffering.

We may not be imprisoned like Paul, but we all face struggles—illness, injustice, rejection, or even fear. What if, like Paul, we saw our pain as a pulpit? What if our hardest moments became megaphones for hope?

Standing for truth and justice in a broken world won't always be easy. But Paul's life reminds us that the mission doesn't stop because of hardship. It often moves forward because of it.

PERSONAL PRAYER:

> Lord Jesus, help me see my struggles through Your eyes. When life feels like it's closing in, remind me that You are still at work. Use my pain to point others to You. Make me bold like Paul, living every moment for Your glory. Amen.

Prayer for the Nation:

Father, we pray for our nation—that in times of division, hardship, and fear, Your gospel would still go forward. Raise up leaders and citizens who live boldly for truth and justice. Let Your light shine through us, even in our struggles. Amen.

Memorable Quote:

"Chains may hold the body, but nothing can lock down the gospel."

Reflection:

1. What current struggle could become a platform for you to share Jesus?
2. How can you encourage someone today to keep going in their mission, despite hardship?
3. Ask God to open your eyes to the people around you who need to see His hope through your life.

Day 28

Faith on Trial

BiblePlan Reading: Acts 24:10–27

Focus: Paul defends himself before rulers, not to escape, but to preach. He remains respectful, truthful, and anchored.

Ponder: Are you willing to speak truth when you're misunderstood or misjudged?

Key Verse(s): *"I am standing before Caesar's court because of the hope of the resurrection of the dead."*—Acts 24:15 (NLT)

When Paul faced trial before Governor Felix, he didn't dodge the accusations or beg for mercy. Instead, he used the opportunity to boldly share his faith and the hope he carried—the resurrection of Jesus and the eternal life it promises. Though misunderstood and misjudged, Paul remained respectful and truthful, anchored in the unshakable truth of the gospel.

This passage shows us a man whose courage wasn't rooted in his circumstances but in his unwavering confidence in God's redemptive plan. Paul understood that standing for truth sometimes means standing alone before those who may not understand or accept you. Yet, his boldness wasn't reckless; it was marked by respect and integrity, a model for how to engage even hostile audiences.

God's character shines through Paul's example—a God who empowers His followers to speak boldly and live with conviction, trusting that truth and justice ultimately prevail. The gospel moves forward not by avoiding trials, but by facing them head-on with grace and courage.

Today, reflect on your own willingness to speak truth when misunderstood. Are you prepared to stand firm in your faith even when it feels like you're on trial? True freedom comes not from avoiding conflict but from anchoring yourself in Christ's truth, allowing His Spirit to guide your words and actions.

PERSONAL PRAYER:

> Lord, give me courage to stand firm in truth even when I'm misunderstood. Help me speak with respect and boldness, anchored in Your love and justice. Let my faith shine through every trial, so others may see Your hope in me. In Jesus' name, Amen.

Prayer for the Nation:

Father, we ask for Your grace over our nation. Raise up believers who will stand boldly for truth, freedom, and justice. When trials come, may we respond with integrity and courage rooted in Your Spirit. Heal divisions and guide our leaders to govern with wisdom and righteousness. In Jesus' name, Amen.

Memorable Quote:

"True freedom is standing firm in truth, even when the world puts your faith on trial."

Reflection:

1. How do I respond when my faith or beliefs are misunderstood or challenged?
2. In what ways can I prepare myself to speak truth with respect and boldness?
3. What does freedom mean to me in the context of faith, and how can I live that out today?

Day 29

Courage in the Chaos

BiblePlan Reading: Acts 27:13–44

Focus: Shipwrecked yet calm, Paul encourages everyone around him. His confidence comes from trusting God's promises.

Ponder: How can you lead others with peace when storms rage?

Key Verse(s): *"But Paul said to the centurion and the soldiers, 'Unless these men stay with the ship, you cannot be saved.'"*—Acts 27:31 (NIV)

In this passage, Paul and his companions are caught in a violent storm at sea, facing what seems like certain disaster. Despite the chaos and fear around him, Paul remains calm and confident, grounded in God's promises. He encourages everyone aboard to hold on, trusting that God will protect them all. His faith doesn't remove the danger, but it transforms how he faces it and how he leads others through it.

This story reveals the steadfast nature of God—His faithfulness even when circumstances are dark and uncertain. God's redemptive plan is not about avoiding hardship but about being present with us through it, giving us peace and courage to stand firm. Paul's boldness comes from knowing God's promises are unshakable, and that truth anchors him amid the storm.

For us today, in a world often filled with chaos and confusion, Paul's example challenges us to lead with calm confidence. Whether standing for truth, justice, or freedom, we must trust God's promises and inspire those around us to hold fast. Spiritual freedom isn't just about being unchained—it's about the courage to face storms without panic, to stand firm in what is right, and to offer peace when fear threatens to overwhelm.

When storms rage around you—whether personal struggles or societal unrest—remember Paul's courage. Trust that God is with you, and be a beacon of peace and hope to those who need it most.

PERSONAL PRAYER:

> Lord, when life feels like a storm, help me to stand firm in Your promises. Give me courage to lead others with peace and hope, even when everything around me feels uncertain. May my faith be a light in the chaos, shining with the freedom found only in You. Amen.

Prayer for the Nation:

God of justice and peace, we pray for our nation in times of unrest and uncertainty. Strengthen leaders and citizens alike to stand courageously for truth and freedom. Calm the storms that divide us, and unite us in Your peace. Let Your promises be our anchor, today and always. Amen.

Memorable Quote:

"True courage isn't the absence of fear—it's trusting God's promises enough to lead through the storm."

Reflection:

1. When have you faced a "storm" in your life where you needed to lead others with peace? How did you respond?
2. What promises of God can you hold onto when fear and uncertainty surround you?
3. How can you encourage someone else today to stand firm in truth and freedom despite the chaos?

Day 30

Preaching Under Guard

BiblePlan Reading: Acts 28:16–31

Focus: Paul lives under house arrest but keeps sharing the gospel—unhindered in spirit.

Ponder: What if your limitations are God's invitations to a new kind of ministry?

Key Verse(s): *"He proclaimed the kingdom of God and taught about the Lord Jesus Christ—with all boldness and without hindrance!"*—Acts 28:31 (NIV)

When Paul finally reached Rome, it wasn't in triumph but in chains. Confined to house arrest and chained to a Roman guard, Paul could've seen his situation as a setback. But instead of focusing on what he couldn't do, Paul leaned into what he still could. The gospel wasn't chained, and neither was his voice.

From that house in Rome, Paul welcomed everyone who came. Jews. Gentiles. Curious seekers. Skeptical neighbors. Soldiers on shift. He preached about the kingdom of God, boldly and without hindrance—because no external limitation could silence his internal fire. In fact, some of his most powerful letters—the "Prison Epistles"—came from this season of confinement.

This passage is a reminder that God's mission doesn't stall when circumstances shift. Sometimes, the most unexpected moments—illness, isolation, canceled plans, or even injustice—become surprising platforms for truth to shine. Paul didn't wait for freedom to speak freely. He chose to be faithful right where he was, even under guard.

God's redemptive plan includes using our limitations for His glory. He turns locked doors into open opportunities. When the world tries to restrict the message of Jesus, God finds a way to amplify it through surrendered hearts like Paul's.

As believers, especially in times when truth is challenged or justice feels far off, we're called to stand firm and speak boldly. Like Paul, we may not always choose our surroundings—but we can always choose our response. And when we do, our boldness becomes a beacon for others, even from behind closed doors.

Personal Prayer:

Lord, help me to see limitations not as roadblocks, but as redirections. Use every season of my life—even the hard and hidden ones—to share Your truth. Fill me with courage to speak boldly, no matter where I am.

Prayer for the Nation:

Father, raise up voices in our nation that speak truth with boldness and grace, even in adversity. Use what seems like limitation or loss to spark revival. Let Your gospel run freely, even when others try to restrain it.

Memorable Quote:

"You can chain a preacher, but you can't chain the gospel."

Reflection:

1. Where do you feel limited right now—and how might God use it for His glory?
2. How can you be bold in your faith today, even in a place or role that feels small?
3. Who has God brought near you, like Paul's visitors, that needs to hear the truth?

Day 31

Strength in Weakness

BiblePlan Reading: 2 Corinthians 12:1–10

Focus: Paul's suffering didn't disappear—but God's power showed up in his weakness.

Ponder: Do you believe God can use your pain to show His strength?

Key Verse(s): *"But he said to me, 'My grace is sufficient for you, for my power is made perfect in weakness.' Therefore I will boast all the more gladly of my weaknesses, so that the power of Christ may rest upon me."*—2 Corinthians 12:9 (ESV)

When we think of freedom fighters and heroes, we imagine people with fierce courage, loud voices, and unshakable strength. But Paul flips that picture upside down. In 2 Corinthians 12, Paul confesses something shocking: his greatest spiritual victories didn't come through his strength—but through his weakness.

Paul had what he called a "thorn in the flesh"—some painful struggle that never left him. He begged God to take it away. But God answered with something better than relief: grace. "My grace is sufficient for you, for My power is made perfect in weakness."

This changes everything. God doesn't always remove the hard things. Sometimes, He uses them to reveal His power. In Paul's case, the thorn didn't disqualify him from ministry—it became the very place where God's power shined the brightest.

As we stand for truth, freedom, and justice, we might feel disqualified—too weak, too tired, too broken. But weakness isn't failure. It's an invitation for God to move. Real strength isn't found in being loud or proud—it's found in letting God work through our surrendered, dependent hearts.

We live in a world that tries to hide weakness and glorify strength. But the gospel tells a better story: *God uses the humble to bring hope, the hurting to display healing, and the broken to reveal beauty.* That's the kind of strength our world desperately needs.

PERSONAL PRAYER:

> Heavenly Father, I don't like feeling weak—but I thank You that Your power shows up when I have none left. Use even the painful places in my life to show Your strength and goodness. Help me trust You more, especially when things don't change the way I hoped. In Jesus' name, Amen.

Prayer for the Nation:

God, in a time when our nation feels weary and divided, we ask for Your grace to be our strength. Show Your power in our weakness. Raise up leaders and citizens who are humble, truthful, and bold—not in their own strength, but in Yours. Let Your power shine through our national struggles. In Jesus' name, Amen.

Memorable Quote:

"Weakness isn't failure—it's an invitation for God's power to show up."

Reflection:

1. What is one area of weakness in your life that God might want to use for His glory?
2. How does depending on God's strength change the way you face challenges or stand for truth?
3. This week, choose one way to rely on God's grace instead of your own strength.

Day 32

Joy No Matter What

BiblePlan Reading: Philippians 4:4–13

Focus: Paul wrote one of the most joy-filled letters from prison. His secret? Christ was enough.

Ponder: Where are you seeking peace or strength apart from Christ?

Key Verse(s): *"I can do all things through Christ who strengthens me."*—Philippians 4:13 (NKJV)

Paul wrote these words from a prison cell—not a cozy cell with visitors and books, but one cold, damp, and chained to guards. And yet his letter to the Philippians overflows with joy. Not circumstantial happiness, but deep-rooted joy that couldn't be shaken by bars, injustice, or hardship. His secret wasn't a positive mindset or a talent for finding silver linings. Paul had learned the secret of contentment in every situation: *Christ was enough.*

He writes, "Rejoice in the Lord always," and he means it. His joy wasn't tied to freedom, health, or public approval. It was tied to a Person. Paul knew that if Christ was with him, *he had everything*. That's why he could say, "I've learned to be content... whether well-fed or hungry... I can do all things through Christ."

This reveals a powerful truth about God: His presence is not limited by our circumstances. Whether on a platform or in a prison, God is there. Whether our nation is thriving or struggling, He is our peace, our strength, and our Provider.

In a world full of noise, pressure, and uncertainty, we're tempted to chase peace through control, popularity, money, or distractions. But none of it satisfies. Only when we let Christ be our strength do we experience the unshakable joy Paul had.

As followers of Jesus—and as "freedom fighters" for truth and justice—our joy is our witness. It's a bold declaration that our hope isn't tied to outcomes or opinions, but anchored in Someone greater. In Christ, we're free from fear and full of joy—even when the world shakes.

PERSONAL PRAYER:

> Lord Jesus, teach me the secret Paul knew—how to rejoice in You no matter what. Help me stop chasing strength in other places and start resting in You. You are enough. Amen.

Prayer for the Nation:

God of freedom and peace, bless this nation with joy that isn't rooted in wealth or power, but in truth and righteousness. Raise up people who shine with hope and contentment in Christ. Let our joy point others to You. Amen.

Memorable Quote:

"Joy isn't the absence of struggle—it's the presence of Christ in the middle of it."

Reflection:

1. Where are you tempted to seek peace or strength apart from Christ?
2. How could choosing joy be a bold witness for truth and freedom in your world today?
3. Memorize Philippians 4:13 and repeat it when you feel weak or overwhelmed.

Day 33

Finishing Strong

BiblePlan Reading: 2 Timothy 4:6–8

Focus: As Paul neared the end, he looked back with no regrets. Faithful. Focused. Ready to meet Jesus.

Ponder: Are you living today in a way you'll be proud of tomorrow?

Key Verse(s): *"I have fought the good fight, I have finished the race, I have kept the faith."*—2 Timothy 4:7 (ESV)

As Paul penned these words to Timothy, he wasn't just saying goodbye—he was testifying. After a lifetime of hardship, beatings, prison time, false accusations, and long, lonely nights, Paul could say without hesitation: *I finished well.* He wasn't perfect, but he had remained faithful. Through it all, he had never stopped believing, never stopped preaching, never stopped hoping. That's the kind of finish we should aim for.

Paul's confidence came from knowing who he had lived for. He didn't run after comfort, applause, or safety—he ran after Christ. And now, at the finish line of his life, he could look forward to the crown of righteousness the Lord had promised him. Not just for him, but "to all who have longed for His appearing." In other words, this isn't just Paul's story. It can be yours too.

We live in a world that pressures us to compromise, stay silent, or give up when things get hard. But finishing the race of faith well means choosing truth even when it's unpopular, walking in freedom even when it's costly, and holding on to Jesus no matter what comes. It's not about having an easy life; it's about living a faithful one.

God is looking for people who, like Paul, are willing to stand up, speak truth, and stay faithful all the way to the end. Heroes of faith aren't always loud or flashy. Sometimes they're quiet, consistent, and bold in the small things—day after day. One day, your life story will be told. Let it be one that says, *I never stopped running toward Jesus.*

PERSONAL PRAYER:

> Jesus, help me live each day with the end in mind. Strengthen me to be faithful in both big and small moments. When I get tired, remind me why I'm running. I want to finish well—for You.

PRAYER FOR THE NATION:

> God of justice and mercy, raise up leaders and citizens who value truth, integrity, and perseverance. May our nation not only start well, but finish well—seeking Your ways in every generation.

MEMORABLE QUOTE:

"A life lived for Christ leaves no regrets at the finish line."

REFLECTION:

1. What choices today will help you finish strong tomorrow?
2. Are you chasing comfort or Christ?
3. How can you stay faithful in the small things this week?

Part 5

JESUS: THE ULTIMATE FREEDOM-GIVER

A 9-Day Journey Through the Life, Death, and Resurrection of Christ

True freedom isn't found in circumstances—it's found in a Savior. Jesus didn't come to start a revolution. He came to set hearts free forever. This devotional invites you to walk through the life of Jesus and discover the full freedom He offers.

Memory Verse:
"So if the Son sets you free, you will be free indeed."
—John 8:36

Day 34

The Promise of Freedom

BiblePlan Reading: Luke 4:16–21

Focus: Jesus declared He came to set captives free. His mission was freedom—spiritual, emotional, and eternal.

Ponder: What areas of your life still feel bound?

Key Verse(s): *"The Spirit of the Lord is on me, because he has anointed me to proclaim good news to the poor. He has sent me to proclaim freedom for the prisoners and recovery of sight for the blind, to set the oppressed free."*— Luke 4:18 (NIV)

When Jesus stood in the synagogue and read from Isaiah, He wasn't just reading ancient prophecy—He was proclaiming His mission. In Luke 4, He makes a bold declaration: *"Today this Scripture is fulfilled in your hearing."* Jesus is the fulfillment of God's promise to rescue, redeem, and restore.

The message is clear: Jesus came to bring freedom. Not the kind that politics or policies can provide, but something deeper and eternal. He came for the poor, the blind, the brokenhearted, the captives—anyone chained by sin, shame, fear, or injustice. The world offers temporary fixes, but Jesus offers transformation from the inside out.

Isaiah's words point to a Savior who binds up wounds, gives beauty for ashes, and turns mourning into praise. This is the heart of our God—one who sees us in our lowest places and steps in to set us free.

Even as believers, we can find ourselves bound by things like anxiety, bitterness, or habits we can't break. But Jesus' mission didn't end in the synagogue—it continued to the cross and through the resurrection. His promise still stands. Where His Spirit is, there is freedom (2 Corinthians 3:17).

As followers of the Ultimate Freedom-Giver, we're also called to carry this mission forward—to proclaim truth, defend the oppressed, and walk in the freedom He offers.

PERSONAL PRAYER:

> Jesus, thank You for coming to set me free. Help me see where I'm still in chains and give me the courage to walk in the freedom You've won. Teach me to live in the power of Your Spirit. Amen.

Prayer for the Nation:

Lord, our nation needs Your freedom. Heal the broken, open blind eyes, and bring justice where there is oppression. Let Your Spirit awaken hearts and transform this land with Your truth and grace. Amen.

Memorable Quote:

"Jesus didn't just promise freedom—He became the freedom we desperately need."

Reflection:

1. What's one area of your life where you need to experience Jesus' freedom?
2. How can you be a voice for truth and healing in a hurting world this week?
3. Ask God to show you someone bound by fear or oppression—and look for a way to encourage or pray for them.

Day 35

Freedom from Shame

BiblePlan Reading: John 4:1–26

Focus: Jesus meets a broken, ashamed woman at the well—and offers her living water and dignity.

Ponder: Are you letting your past define your present?

Key Verse(s): *"Then, leaving her water jar, the woman went back to the town and said to the people, 'Come, see a man who told me everything I ever did. Could this be the Messiah?'"*—John 4:28–29 (NIV)

Jesus didn't go around Samaria—He went straight through it. That wasn't the usual route for Jewish travelers, especially devout ones. But Jesus had an appointment with a woman at a well—one the world had already dismissed. She was drawing water in the heat of the day, likely trying to avoid the judging eyes of her community. Her shame hung over her like the blazing sun.

But Jesus saw her. Not just her shame or her story, but her soul. In a few words, He uncovered her past—not to humiliate her, but to invite her into something better. Living water. New life. True freedom.

This moment at the well reminds us that Jesus is not afraid of our messy pasts. He walks straight into them, offering dignity where others offer labels, hope where others offer judgment. He doesn't define us by our worst decisions—He redefines us through grace.

In a culture where shame shouts loudly and cancel culture reigns, Jesus stands as the freedom-giver. He confronts lies with truth and meets our guilt with mercy. For the woman at the well, that encounter changed everything. Her shame turned into a story. Her fear became a testimony. She ran back to the very people she once avoided, declaring the good news.

If Jesus could restore her, He can restore you. Let His voice be louder than your shame. And in a world quick to condemn, be someone who, like Jesus, speaks truth with love and offers dignity to the broken. That's how freedom spreads. That's how justice begins.

PERSONAL PRAYER:

> Jesus, thank You for seeing me beyond my past. Wash away the shame I carry and fill me with Your living water. Help me to walk in the freedom You've given and share it with others who feel unseen and unworthy.

Prayer for the Nation:

Lord, we pray for a nation heavy with shame and division. Let Your truth and grace run like rivers through our land. Heal wounds, restore dignity, and raise up people who stand for justice, truth, and the freedom only You can give.

Memorable Quote:

"Jesus doesn't define us by our worst decisions—He redefines us through grace."

Reflection:

1. Are there areas in your life where shame still holds power?
2. How can you extend dignity to someone who feels cast aside?
3. Who needs to hear your story of how Jesus set you free?

Day 36

Freedom from Religion

BiblePlan Reading: Matthew 11:28–30

Focus: Jesus invites the weary—not into more rules—but into rest. His yoke is easy because His love is deep.

Ponder: Are you living to be accepted, or living from acceptance in Christ?

Key Verse(s): *"Come to me, all who labor and are heavy laden, and I will give you rest. Take my yoke upon you, and learn from me, for I am gentle and lowly in heart, and you will find rest for your souls. For my yoke is easy, and my burden is light."* —Matthew 11:28–30

We don't usually think of religion as something we need freedom *from*. But Jesus saw how religious systems were crushing people. The Pharisees had created a culture of endless rules—where worth was earned, not received. Faith became more about performing than trusting, more about fear than freedom. But Jesus broke through with a different call: *Come to Me.*

In this invitation, we see the heart of God. Jesus doesn't ask the weary to work harder—He offers them rest. His yoke isn't a new set of demands, but a relationship. It's walking with Him, learning from Him, and being held by His grace. His "burden" is light because His love carries what we can't.

This is the freedom Jesus gives: freedom from trying to earn God's approval. Freedom from the shame of not measuring up. Freedom from the exhausting cycle of doing more to be enough. We don't live *for* acceptance—we live *from* it. That's what makes His yoke easy: it's love, not law, that leads us.

When we live this way, we become people who fight for others' freedom too. Not by judging or controlling, but by lifting burdens and pointing to Jesus. As believers, our stand for truth and justice must be rooted in grace. We fight not to oppress with rules but to set captives free—with the same mercy that set us free.

PERSONAL PRAYER:

> Jesus, thank You that I don't have to earn Your love. I bring You my tired heart and my heavy burdens. Teach me to walk with You, rest in You, and live in the freedom You've already given.

Prayer for the Nation:

Lord, break the grip of performance-based religion in our land. Heal the hurt caused by empty rituals and prideful systems. Raise up a generation that walks in Your grace and leads with love. May Your rest be known from coast to coast.

Memorable Quote:

"Jesus didn't come to burden the broken—He came to carry them."

Reflection:

1. Are you living to be accepted, or living from acceptance in Christ?
2. Where in your life have you confused religion with relationship?
3. This week, look for one way to lift a burden from someone else—with grace, not guilt.

Day 37

Freedom from Fear

BiblePlan Reading: Mark 4:35–41

Focus: Jesus calms a raging storm with a word. His power brings peace even in chaos.

Ponder: What fears are keeping you from trusting Him fully?

Key Verse(s): *"He got up, rebuked the wind and said to the waves, 'Quiet! Be still!' Then the wind died down and it was completely calm."*—Mark 4:39 (NIV)

Jesus had just finished teaching the crowds when He told His disciples to get in the boat and cross the lake. But partway across, a violent storm struck. The wind roared. Waves crashed. The disciples—some of them seasoned fishermen—panicked. And Jesus? He was asleep. In fear, they shook Him awake: "Don't you care if we drown?"

Jesus didn't panic. He didn't even rise with alarm. He stood, spoke three simple words—*"Quiet! Be still!"*—and the chaos obeyed. The storm stopped. Just like that. And then, He asked them, "Why are you so afraid? Do you still have no faith?"

This moment reveals not only Jesus' power over nature, but something even deeper—His heart for our peace. The storm was real. The danger was real. But so was His presence. Jesus never promised a life free from storms. But He does promise to be with us in them—and to bring peace that fear can't steal.

Spiritual freedom doesn't always mean freedom from difficulty. Sometimes, it means freedom *in* difficulty—freedom from fear, anxiety, and despair. That kind of peace comes only from knowing who is in the boat with you. When we stand for truth, freedom, and justice in a world that often feels chaotic, it's easy to feel overwhelmed. But Jesus hasn't left us alone. He's not asleep at the wheel. He's still Lord of the storm.

Let this truth anchor your soul: Jesus is stronger than your storm. You don't have to let fear rule your choices. Stand firm in faith. Speak truth with courage. And remember—when He speaks, even the wind and waves obey.

PERSONAL PRAYER:

> Lord Jesus, I confess that fear sometimes gets the best of me. But You are stronger than anything I face. Speak peace over

my heart and help me trust that You're in control, even when things feel out of control. I choose faith over fear because I know You are with me. Amen.

Prayer for the Nation:

Father, our country faces many storms—division, injustice, uncertainty. We ask You to rise and speak peace over our land. Calm the chaos. Awaken our leaders and people to Your presence. Let Your justice roll like a river, and Your peace settle in every heart. In Jesus' Name, Amen.

Memorable Quote:

"Spiritual freedom isn't found in the absence of storms—but in knowing who is in the boat with you."

Reflection:

1. What fear do you need to surrender to Jesus today?
2. How can remembering Jesus' power help you take a bold step for truth or justice this week?
3. Spend time imagining Jesus standing in your storm and saying, "Peace, be still." What changes in you when you believe it?

Day 38

Freedom from Sin's Grip

BiblePlan Reading: John 8:1–11

Focus: A woman caught in sin is forgiven, not condemned. Jesus offers mercy with the call to change.

Ponder: Are you still carrying guilt Jesus already took?

Key Verse(s): *"Then neither do I condemn you,"* Jesus declared. *"Go now and leave your life of sin."*—John 8:11b (NIV)

A woman was dragged before Jesus, caught in the act of adultery. Her accusers clutched stones, quoting the Law, ready to end her life with judgment. But Jesus—calm, righteous, and full of truth—stooped down and wrote in the dust. Then He looked up and said, *"Let any one of you who is without sin be the first to throw a stone."* One by one, they dropped their stones and walked away.

Jesus didn't ignore the woman's sin—but neither did He condemn her. Instead, He gave her freedom. Freedom from shame. Freedom from death. Freedom to live differently.

This scene reveals the heart of God's redemptive plan: mercy without compromise. Jesus never excuses sin, but He refuses to chain us to it. He confronts us with truth and then offers us grace—a clean start. That's real freedom. Not the right to keep doing wrong, but the power to walk away from what once held us.

In a world quick to cancel, judge, and shame, Jesus shows us a different way: He speaks truth and gives hope. If you're still carrying guilt for something Jesus already died to forgive, it's time to let it go. Receive His mercy—and leave behind the weight of your past.

As freedom fighters in today's world, we must reflect Christ's balance of truth and grace. Stand against sin, yes—but also stoop beside the broken. We fight for justice not just by exposing wrongs, but by helping people find the way out of them.

Personal Prayer:

> Jesus, thank You for not condemning me. You see my sin and yet offer mercy. Help me to leave behind the guilt and walk in the freedom You purchased for me. Change my heart and make me more like You.

PRAYER FOR THE NATION:

> Lord, have mercy on our land. Forgive us where we've traded justice for judgment and truth for convenience. Raise up leaders and citizens who speak truth with grace, who champion mercy without compromise. Heal our wounds and free us from sin's grip.

MEMORABLE QUOTE:

"Jesus doesn't excuse sin—He breaks its power and sets us free to live differently."

REFLECTION:

1. Are you still carrying guilt Jesus has already forgiven? Why?
2. Who needs to hear words of truth and grace from you today?
3. How can you reflect Jesus by standing for both justice and mercy this week?

Day 39

Freedom through the Cross

BiblePlan Reading: Luke 23:26–49

Focus: Jesus died as our substitute, paying the full price for our freedom. The cross isn't defeat—it's deliverance.

Ponder: Do you truly believe Jesus' sacrifice was enough for your worst moments?

Key Verse(s): "Jesus called out with a loud voice, 'Father, into your hands I commit my spirit.' When he had said this, he breathed his last."—Luke 23:46 (NIV)

When Jesus carried the cross to Golgotha, it seemed like the end—defeat and shame. But the truth of that day runs deeper than any earthly pain or injustice. Jesus died not as a victim, but as a willing substitute, paying the full price for our freedom. In those final hours, He bore the weight of our sins and the consequences of a broken world so that we might be free—free from guilt, slavery to sin, and the fear of death itself.

This passage reveals the heart of God's redemptive plan: freedom through sacrifice. Jesus' death on the cross was not a tragic loss but the ultimate act of love and justice. He stood for truth, even when it cost Him everything. His surrender was a victory over the powers of darkness that hold us captive.

What does this mean for you today? It means that no matter what your "worst moments" are—your failures, regrets, or fears—Jesus' sacrifice covers it all. Freedom isn't just a future promise; it is a present reality. When we accept His death as our substitute, we are empowered to stand for truth and justice boldly, knowing we are no longer bound by shame or condemnation.

As we celebrate freedom in our nation, let us also remember the greater freedom purchased on the cross—a freedom that transforms hearts and restores hope. Let this truth fuel your courage to be a freedom fighter in your own sphere, standing for what is right and true because Jesus has already won the victory.

PERSONAL PRAYER:

> Jesus, thank You for carrying my burdens and paying the price for my freedom. Help me to live each day in the power of Your sacrifice, standing for truth and justice without fear. Teach me to trust fully in Your redeeming love, especially when I feel weak or unworthy. In Your name, Amen.

PRAYER FOR THE NATION:

Lord, we ask that Your freedom and truth would shine brightly over this nation. Heal our divisions and empower us to stand united for justice and righteousness. May the sacrifice of Jesus inspire us all to pursue true liberty—not just politically, but spiritually—so we may live as a people set free by Your grace. Amen.

MEMORABLE QUOTE:

"The cross is not defeat; it is the victory that sets us free."

REFLECTION:

1. How does knowing Jesus died as your substitute change the way you view your past mistakes or failures?
2. In what ways can you stand for truth and justice in your community, inspired by Jesus' example on the cross?
3. Reflect on areas in your life where you still feel bound or burdened—how can you surrender these to Jesus and embrace the freedom He offers?

Day 40

Freedom through Resurrection

BiblePlan Reading: Luke 24:1–12

Focus: The grave couldn't hold Him. His victory is our freedom from death and despair.

Ponder: How does the resurrection give you hope right now?

Key Verse(s): *"He is not here; he has risen! Remember how he told you, while he was still with you in Galilee."*—Luke 24:6 (NIV)

The empty tomb is the ultimate symbol of victory—Jesus conquered death and rose again, proving that no grave, no darkness, no despair can hold down the One who is Life itself. Luke 24 opens with the women arriving at Jesus' tomb, expecting to anoint a lifeless body, only to find the stone rolled away and angels proclaiming the good news: He is risen! This resurrection confirms God's power over death and His unstoppable plan to bring redemption to the world.

This moment reveals the heart of God's redemptive plan: freedom. Jesus' resurrection isn't just a miraculous event for history's sake; it's the foundation of our spiritual freedom. Because He lives, we are freed from the fear of death, freed from the chains of despair, and freed to live boldly in truth and justice. The resurrection gives us a hope that transcends every struggle—personal, societal, or national.

In standing for truth and justice, the resurrection reminds us that darkness will not have the final word. Even when the world seems broken or corrupt, Jesus' victory assures us that God's justice will prevail. We fight not as those defeated but as freedom fighters empowered by the risen King.

Right now, whatever challenges or doubts you face, the resurrection invites you to hold fast to hope. Jesus' rising means new beginnings, healing, and courage to stand for what is right—even when it's costly.

PERSONAL PRAYER:

Jesus, thank You for rising from the grave and giving me freedom from fear and despair. Help me to live each day with the boldness and hope Your resurrection brings. When I feel weak or overwhelmed, remind me that You have already won. Empower me to stand for truth and justice in my world. In Your name, Amen.

Prayer for the Nation:

Lord, as we celebrate freedom, we ask for Your resurrection power to breathe new life into our nation. Heal our divisions, strengthen our leaders with wisdom, and inspire Your people to seek truth and justice. May Your victory over death be the foundation for lasting peace and freedom in our land. Amen.

Memorable Quote:

"The empty tomb declares that no darkness can hold down the light of truth and freedom."

Reflection:

1. How does knowing Jesus rose from the dead change the way you face your daily challenges?
2. In what ways can you stand for truth and justice today, empowered by the hope of the resurrection?
3. What fears or doubts can you surrender to Jesus' victorious power right now?

Day 41

Freedom to Live Changed

BiblePlan Reading: John 20:19–22

Focus: The risen Jesus sends His followers to live boldly—with His Spirit and peace.

Ponder: Are you walking in the freedom Jesus already gave you?

Key Verse(s): *"Again Jesus said, 'Peace be with you! As the Father has sent me, I am sending you.'"* — John 20:21

When Jesus appeared to His disciples after His resurrection, they were hiding—locked behind closed doors, afraid and uncertain. But the risen Christ didn't just come to comfort them; He came to transform them. He greeted them with peace—*not just the absence of conflict, but a deep, unshakable peace rooted in His presence.* Then He empowered them by breathing the Holy Spirit into them and commissioning them to go out into the world boldly.

This moment reveals the heart of God's redemptive plan: freedom is more than escaping fear or chains—it's living changed, filled with Spirit-empowered courage to stand for truth and justice. Jesus gives peace and power together so His followers can live out their calling as freedom fighters in a world still often hostile to truth.

Do you recognize the freedom Jesus has already given you? Like the disciples, you might sometimes feel locked behind fear or doubt. But Jesus invites you to receive His Spirit and step out in peace, courage, and purpose. Every act of standing up for truth, defending justice, and loving others boldly flows from that same Spirit. Your freedom isn't just personal—it's meant to be lived out, shining light in the darkest places.

Let today be a reminder: You don't walk alone. Jesus breathes life and power into you, sending you forth to live changed and free.

PERSONAL PRAYER:

> Jesus, thank You for the peace You bring and the Spirit You give. Help me to live boldly in the freedom You've won—standing for truth, justice, and love without fear. Fill me anew with Your power and courage today. Amen.

Prayer for the Nation:

Father, we pray for our nation—that Your Spirit would empower us to live out freedom with responsibility and courage. Heal the fears and divisions that lock hearts away. May Your peace lead us to justice, truth, and unity. Amen.

Memorable Quote:

"True freedom is living boldly, empowered by the Spirit and anchored in Christ's peace."

Reflection:

1. In what areas of your life do you still feel "locked behind closed doors" of fear or doubt? How can you invite Jesus to breathe His Spirit into those places?
2. How does knowing Jesus sends you with His peace and power change the way you approach standing for truth and justice?
3. What practical step can you take today to live more boldly as a freedom fighter in your community?

Day 42

Freedom That Lasts Forever

BiblePlan Reading: Revelation 1:12–18

Focus: Jesus is alive and reigning. The freedom He gives now will one day be complete.

Ponder: How can living with eternity in mind change how you live today?

Key Verse(s): *"I am the First and the Last. I am the Living One; I was dead, and now look, I am alive forever and ever! And I hold the keys of death and Hades."*—Revelation 1:17b-18 (NIV)

In this powerful vision, the Apostle John sees Jesus not as a distant figure but as the Living One—alive forever, victorious over death and holding ultimate authority. Jesus declares Himself as the "First and the Last," the beginning and the end of all things. His resurrection is not just a past event; it is the foundation for our present hope and future freedom. Because Jesus conquered death, the freedom He offers isn't temporary or conditional—it's eternal.

Freedom Fighters: Heroes of Faith Who Stood for Truth

This passage reminds us that our fight for truth, justice, and freedom today is part of a larger, divine story. Jesus reigns with authority over all creation, and His victory assures us that injustice and oppression will not have the final word. The freedom we experience now—freedom from sin, fear, and condemnation—is a foretaste of the full freedom we will enjoy when Christ returns to establish His perfect kingdom.

Living with eternity in mind transforms how we stand for truth today. We don't fight for freedom out of despair or anger but with confident hope in Jesus' ultimate victory. This hope empowers us to pursue justice courageously, love sacrificially, and hold fast to truth even when it costs us. Because Jesus is alive and reigning, our efforts are never in vain. We are called to be freedom fighters—reflecting His character, sharing His truth, and embodying His love until that day when all will be made new.

PERSONAL PRAYER:

Jesus, thank You for conquering death and giving me freedom that lasts forever. Help me to live each day with eternity in mind, standing boldly for Your truth and justice. Strengthen me to reflect Your love and courage in a world that desperately needs Your hope. Amen.

Prayer for the Nation:

Lord, we ask You to guide our nation with Your truth and justice. May we remember that true freedom comes from You alone. Inspire our leaders and citizens alike to seek Your wisdom and walk in Your ways, so that freedom, peace, and righteousness may flourish in our land. Amen.

Memorable Quote:

"Because Jesus is alive, our fight for freedom is never without hope—our victory is already won."

Reflection:

1. How does knowing Jesus is alive and reigning change your perspective on challenges you face today?
2. In what ways can you stand for truth and justice with hope rather than fear?
3. What practical steps can you take this week to reflect Jesus' freedom to others around you?

Epilogue

Your Turn to Stand

The pages are finished, but the story isn't.

Moses stood before Pharaoh. Esther stood before a king. Daniel stood in the face of lions. Paul stood in chains. Jesus stood on a cross—and then rose in victory. Each of them stepped into the battle of their generation, not because it was easy, but because it was right. They didn't wait until they were ready. They simply obeyed.

Now, it's your turn.

You may not wear a crown or hold a staff or write letters from prison, but make no mistake—you've been placed in this time for a reason. The same God who called them is calling you to stand for truth in your own corner of the world. To speak life in a culture of confusion. To shine light in a time of compromise. To love fiercely, live humbly, and walk boldly in the freedom Christ has already won.

The world needs people who won't just admire faith heroes—but become one.
Not perfect. Not fearless. Just faithful.

So as you close this book, don't close your heart.

Let what you've read awaken what God has already placed inside you.

Let their courage become your call.

Let their prayers become your posture.

Let their stand become your story.

You were born for such a time as this.

Now rise—and fight the good fight of faith!

Also by BiblePlan Devotionals

Hope in the End: A 31-Day Journey Through the End-Times

Are we living in the last days? What does Bible prophecy really mean — and why does it matter?

<u>Hope in the End</u> is a 31-day devotional that invites you to explore the End-Times through the lens of Scripture, not with fear or confusion, but with clarity, purpose, and unshakable hope. Rooted in the truth of God's Word, this devotional walks you through key end-time passages from Revelation, Daniel, the Gospels, and more — all pointing to one central figure: Jesus Christ, our soon-coming King.

Each daily reading includes:

- A focused Scripture passage
- A devotional reflection that reveals God's heart and plan
- A heartfelt prayer

Whether you're new to Bible prophecy or have studied it for years, **Hope in the End** will renew your vision of Christ's glory and prepare your heart to live with watchful faith, holy obedience, and confident expectation.

This isn't just a study of what's coming — it's a call to live differently *now*. **The end of the story is not darkness — it's hope. And that hope has a name: Jesus.**

Let this devotional strengthen your faith, steady your soul, and stir your heart to live every day in light of eternity.